Creative Decision Making

Using Positive Uncertainty

Revised Edition

H.B. Gelatt and Carol Gelatt

A Fifty-Minute™ Series Book

Creative Decision Making

Using Positive Uncertainty

Revised Edition

H.B. Gelatt and Carol Gelatt

CREDITS:
Senior Editor: **Debbie Woodbury**
Editor: **Ann Gosch**
Assistant Editor: **Genevieve Del Rosario**
Production Manager: **Judy Petry**
Design: **Nicole Phillips**
Production Artist: **Rich Lehl**

ISBN 1-56052-690-4
Library of Congress Catalog Card Number 2003101470
Printed in Canada by Webcom Limited

3 4 5 PM 06 05 04

Learning Objectives For:

CREATIVE DECISION MAKING

The objectives for *Creative Decision Making, Revised Edition,* are listed below. They have been developed to guide you, the reader, to the core issues covered in this book.

THE OBJECTIVES OF THIS BOOK ARE:

- ❏ 1) To explain the four paradoxical principles of positive uncertainty

- ❏ 2) To provide a holistic, *both and more* perspective on creative decision-making

- ❏ 3) To help readers understand that the way they see things is the way they *choose* to see things

- ❏ 4) To demonstrate how to engage in future thinking

ASSESSING YOUR PROGRESS

In addition to the learning objectives above, Course Technology has developed a Crisp Series **assessment** that covers the fundamental information presented in this book. A 25-item, multiple-choice and true/false questionnaire allows the reader to evaluate his or her comprehension of the subject matter. To buy the assessment and answer key, go to www.courseilt.com and search on the book title or via the assessment format, or call 1-800-442-7477.

Assessments should not be used in any employee selection process.

About the Authors

For most of his career, H.B. Gelatt has been passionate about writing and speaking on the topic of decision making. After earning his doctorate in counseling psychology at Stanford, H.B. developed a nationally recognized model of rational decision making. But by 1990 he shifted his focus to creative decision making using *positive uncertainty*. The turning point for this change came when Crisp Learning published the first edition of this book in 1991.

H.B. continues to speak and write about positive uncertainty for people in transition, career development professionals, coaches, counselors, and educators. For information about positive uncertainty workshops and speeches or to share your comments about the book, please contact H.B. by phone at (650) 967-8345, by e-mail at Hb@gelattpartners.com, or check out H.B. and Carol's Web site at www.gelattpartners.com.

Throughout her career, Carol Gelatt has dedicated herself to helping individuals and organizations change, grow, and succeed. As an organizational consultant and executive coach, she continues that mission. Before establishing her own business in 2001, Carol developed a track record of success in senior management, consulting, coaching, and career development. She was an executive in two Internet start-ups, a senior manager and consultant for one of the world's largest career and change management consulting firms, and the founding director of a career development center.

For information about how positive uncertainty is applied in organizations and with individuals and groups, please contact Carol by phone at (650) 960-1922, by e-mail at carol@gelattpartners.com, or check out Carol and H.B.'s Web site at www.gelattpartners.com.

How to Use This Book

A Crisp Learning *Fifty-Minute*™ *Book* can be used in variety of ways. Individual self-study is one of the most common. However, many organizations use *Fifty-Minute* books for pre-study before a classroom training session. Other organizations use the books as a part of a system-wide learning program—supported by video and other media based on the content in the books. Still others work with Crisp Learning to customize the material to meet their specific needs and reflect their culture. Regardless of how it is used, we hope you will join the more than 20 million satisfied learners worldwide who have completed a *Fifty-Minute Book*.

Preface

The first edition of *Creative Decision Making: Using Positive Uncertainty* was published in 1991. This was before chaos was commonly known as the name of a new science of uncertainty and before *emotional intelligence* was redefining what it means to be smart. It was before the prevailing language of popular literature and a growing number of discussion groups throughout the world included terms such as interconnectedness, consciousness, and spirituality.

Many changes have been taking place during the past decade, gradually changing the way we think about things and the way we make decisions. Change itself has been changing. Today change is more rapid, more complex, and more unpredictable than ever before. And two major revolutions are changing our world and the way we see it.

The Internet revolution is changing the way we see the world "out there"–the workplace, store, home, family, human relationships, geographic boundaries, and so on. This revolution has created a desire and a need for more information and more speed. Another revolution is the rapidly increasing focus on looking inside ourselves for understanding of what is happening outside us. Jean Houston named this the Inner-Net Revolution. It is changing the way we see the world "in here." It says to many people that what goes on outside us is interconnected with and partly determined by what goes on inside us. This revolution is creating a growing desire and a need for more reflection and more creative imagination.

We point this out because we believe that *Creative Decision Making: Using Positive Uncertainty* is even more relevant today than when it was first published in 1991. And it is now more likely to be accepted as "new conventional wisdom" about decision making.

Understanding that uncertainty is certain and that it means opportunity is still a theme of this book. Accepting uncertainty without being paralyzed by it is still an objective. We believe that the current rapidity of change and the powerful impact of the "outside" and "inside" revolutions have made this theme more acceptable and the objective more necessary than ever before. What you can do when you do not know what the future will be is to learn to decide creatively with positive uncertainty.

Creative Decision Making: Using Positive Uncertainty is written for individuals who are struggling to make decisions about their careers, relationships, retirement, life, and more. Coaches, trainers, counselors, and educators who advise and teach about the challenges of making career and life decisions will want to add positive uncertainty to their professional toolkit. Teams, managers, and executives will find new resources to help them make decisions about their work and their organization's future.

This revision has an additional perspective because it has a co-author—Carol Gelatt. We are marriage partners and career partners and now we are writing partners. We hope you enjoy reading *Creative Decision Making: Using Positive Uncertainty* as much as we enjoyed writing it!

H.B. Gelatt

Carol Gelatt

Acknowledgments

Special thanks to Shelley Casey, Hannah Chan, Marianne Clark, Betsy Collard, Jean Lawrence, Dana Marks, Joanne Martens, and Marianne Minor for their review and feedback of early versions of the manuscript. Their friendship and support encouraged us and helped keep us on track.

We especially appreciate and are grateful for all of our clients, workshop participants, and audiences at speeches in different parts of the world. They teach us so much about being positive in the face of uncertainty and being creative and bold when deciding. Without them, we would not have a book.

Contents

Introduction: The What and Why of Positive Uncertainty

Are You Ready for Positive Uncertainty? 3

What Is Positive Uncertainty? 4

Why Be Positive About Uncertainty? 5

Getting Started with *Creative Decision Making* 6

Part 1: Paradoxical Principle #1

Be Focused and Flexible About What You Want 9

Identify Barriers to Knowing What You Want 11

Use Goals to Guide You, Not Govern You 12

Take Your Eye Off the Target 14

Treat Goals as Hypotheses 17

Uncover Future Phobia 18

Mine Goals from Past and Future Events 21

Clarify the Big and Little Things You Want 22

Postscript 27

Part 2: Paradoxical Principle #2

Be Aware and Wary of What You Know 31

Question the Validity of Information You Receive 33

More Information Can Cause More Uncertainty 35

Case Study: Coffee Culture 36

Watch Out for Info-Mania 38

Open Your Mind to New Knowledge 39

Expand Your Thinking About Other Possibilities 40

Postscript 47

Part 3: Paradoxical Principle #3

Be Realistic and Optimistic About What You Believe 51

Recognize That Reality Is in the Mind of the Beholder 53

Be Wary of Your Dogma 56

Perceive Perspective Paralysis 57

Treat Beliefs as Prophecy 58

Dream Precisely to Create a Positive Future 60

Uncover Your Beliefs Through Metaphor 61

Explore Your Personal Metaphor 63

Use Scenario Rehearsal in Decision Making 64

Postscript 69

Part 4: Paradoxical Principle #4

Be Practical and Magical About What You Do 73

Treat Intuition as Intelligence 75

Become Aware of Your Decision Strategies 76

Recognize Reverse Paranoia 81

Learn to Plan and Plan to Learn 82

Visualize Outcomes with Decision Trees 84

See the Bigger Picture in Outcomes Windows 85

Postscript 91

Summary

Actions for Practice 95

The Perennial Decision-Making Question 97

Positive Uncertainty Exercises 98

Recommended Reading 110

The What and Why of Positive Uncertainty

2

Are You Ready for Positive Uncertainty?

So much has already been written about creativity and decision making that you probably feel you know that territory. But are you ready to embrace such a concept as *positive uncertainty?* Not much has been written about it so it is unfamiliar and may make you a little uncomfortable (unless you have read the 1991 edition of this book). Yet you probably already possess some of the skills promoted by positive uncertainty.

Answer *yes* or *no* to the following questions to see if you are ready for positive uncertainty. This is not a test. You can continue reading no matter how you answer the questions. It is intended as a preview of what is to come.

Have you ever...

1. Wanted something, gotten it, and found out you wanted something else?	Yes	No
2. Set a clear goal and discovered a better one along the way?	Yes	No
3. Had thoughts that were not completely rational?	Yes	No
4. Found it advantageous not to know something?	Yes	No
5. Had unrealistic fantasies about your future?	Yes	No
6. Experienced a self-fulfilling prophecy?	Yes	No
7. Decided not to decide?	Yes	No
8. Made up your mind and then changed it?	Yes	No

If you answered *yes* to any of these questions, you are ready for positive uncertainty. If you answered *yes* to every question, you are ready and able!

Most people do answer *yes* to most of these questions. Being nonrational, unrealistic, changeable, and uncertain seems to be common practice.

Positive uncertainty encourages you to have some thoughts that are not completely rational, to develop some unrealistic illusions, to become as changeable as your environment, and to be positive about not knowing.

Most schools in the past did not teach these skills, and teachers even discouraged students from using them. In fact, traditional decision-making advice did not include these capabilities. Until recently, most decision strategies preached primarily rational, realistic, systematic, and even scientific practices.

What Is Positive Uncertainty?

Positive uncertainty can be thought of as a philosophy of creative decision making. It is an approach to making any decision—career, relationships, finances, and retirement—about anything significant in your life.

Decision making is defined as using what you *know* and what you *believe* so you can choose what to *do* to get what you *want*. Of course, what you *do* does not always get you what you *want*. Outcomes are uncertain because the future is unpredictable. That inevitable uncertainty between what you do and what you get is what traditional decision strategies try to eliminate with rational processes.

Positive uncertainty, on the other hand, does not prescribe decision rules for choosing. It offers a "point-of-view" as a guide for making creative decisions when the future is uncertain—and the future is always uncertain. It suggests that you acknowledge this uncertainty and be positive about it.

Mark Twain once said, "There are only two things you need to be successful in life: ignorance and confidence." Having ignorance and confidence sounds like being uncertain and positive. Together they are a *paradox*—a contradictory statement that nevertheless may be true. Positive uncertainty contradicts conventional decision-making wisdom, yet there is truth to be found in it.

Why Be Positive About Uncertainty?

Being positive about uncertainty increases possibilities and produces the opportunity for proactive creativity. If the future is certain, all you can do is prepare for it. When the future is uncertain, however, there are lots of possible futures. You can be part of creating the future rather than just preparing for it.

All possibilities exist in the future. Thus, the future is an essential part of decision making. There are three kinds of futures:

Possible futures—what could happen

Probable futures—what is likely to happen

Preferable futures—what you prefer to happen

It could be considered wise decision making to "know" as many of these futures as you can, but decision-makers usually focus on the probable and preferable futures. This focus blocks out the infinite possible futures. With all the limitations on decision making, however, it is a great advantage to increase possibilities.

That is what positive uncertainty is all about: increasing possibilities. When you are absolutely certain (in your mind) about what will happen next, then that is the only thing you can think of happening. But when you are uncertain (in your mind) about what will happen next, you are able to think about additional possibilities. As political columnist and educator Max Lerner advised, "Do not be a pessimist or an optimist; be a 'possibilist.'"

No one can "know" all of these futures because of what has been labeled the *limited rationality* of humans. Decision-makers' goals and preferences are seldom complete or consistent; people keep expanding or changing what they want. Decision-makers seldom consider all the alternatives and consequences. This is what is meant by limited rationality. Even in an information society and with the Internet, we almost never know all we need to know to make a completely rational choice. And even if we did know everything, we do not have the cognitive capability (brainpower) to process it all rationally and rapidly. Plus, we often do not have the willpower to overcome the influence of our subjective mind.

This may sound like bad news, but wait—there is good news.

The good news is that people are naturally creative decision-makers because of humans' *unlimited creativity*. Positive uncertainty recognizes limited rationality and unlimited creativity and promotes creative decision making.

Uncertainty is real; it probably can never be avoided. Accepting this uncertainty and being positive about it opens up possibilities for creative decision making—which is what this book is about.

Getting Started with
Creative Decision Making

Creative Decision Making presents four easy-to-remember paradoxical principles, a few of Murphy's Laws, and profound quotes from well-known sages. It also provides you with strategies and exercises for creating your own rules for deciding. Also included are examples to illustrate a strategy or an exercise.

The four paradoxical principles of positive uncertainty are explained in separate sections in the order that seems "rational"—what you *want, know, believe,* and *do.* But of course they are not separate, and decision making is not always (if ever) performed in a linear, rational, orderly fashion. This means you could read the four principles in any order. They are:

1. Be Focused and Flexible About What You Want

➤ This principle will help you create your goals and discover new ones.

➤ What you want now may not be what you want then.

2. Be Aware and Wary of What You Know

➤ This principle will help you appraise knowing and appreciate not knowing.

➤ What you know may need to become unknown.

3. Be Realistic and Optimistic About What You Believe

➤ This principle will help you realize that your beliefs influence your reality and your behavior.

➤ Believing is seeing is doing.

4. Be Practical and Magical About What You Do

➤ This principle will help you use both your head and your heart in deciding.

➤ What you do to decide is up to you; just do it.

Think of this book as your personal decision-making reference guide that you can return to at any time. The Summary includes exercises that you can use over and over when faced with making career and life decisions.

Paradoxical

Principle #1

This principle will help you both create your goals and discover new ones. What you want now may not be what you want then.

Be Focused and Flexible About What You Want

> " *The only thing worse than not getting what you want, is getting it.*"

–George Bernard Shaw

Much has been written about being focused on your objective in making decisions. The conventional wisdom of rational decision strategy is to identify clear, precise goals and focus on them. This strategy is not obsolete; it is incomplete.

Focusing on a clear, precise goal helps you concentrate on your target. You do not get distracted or sidetracked easily. But concentrating on a goal may also be harmful because it prevents you from getting sidetracked to other potentially desirable goals. Getting sidetracked means taking side roads, off the direct route on your life's journey.

Focusing only on the destination can program your mind too narrowly, cause you to miss the journey, overlook other unanticipated destinations, and block your nonrational, intuitive tendencies. If it is true that life is a journey, not a destination, why do we insist on focusing on the destination?

David Campbell best illustrates the focused approach with the title of his best-selling career guidance book, *If You Don't Know Where You're Going, You'll Probably End up Somewhere Else*. But a Gelatt corollary illustrates the need for flexibility: "If you always know where you're going, you may never end up somewhere else." *Somewhere else* may be where you wanted to go but did not know it. Sometimes the reason for your action might be to find out where you want to go.

Adult vs. Childhood Decision Making

Having a goal before you start out makes sense. Classical decision theory holds that purpose should come before action. In this "adult model" of decision making, adults study alternatives and take action to come as close as possible to achieving their goals. In the "childhood model" of decision making, however, we tell children to do things they *do not want* to do because we believe it will broaden their experiences, expand their interests, and perhaps lead to new goals (James G. March, Stanford professor of education). "Try your vegetables; you might learn to like them." "Piano lessons will be good for you." "You must take three years of math even if you don't want to."

In one decision model it is assumed adults already know what they want; in the other model it is assumed children do not. Classical decision theory (the adult model) tells us how to make good decisions but not how to find good goals. Positive uncertainty's Paradoxical Principle #1—be focused and flexible about what you want—employs both the adult and childhood model: a *both and more* perspective.

Positive uncertainty encourages you to use both the adult model and the childhood model of decision making and more. Sometimes what you want is so powerful you just know it. But being tentative, creative, and open-minded when defining what you want will increase the number of possible futures for you to explore. Have the courage of your convictions but also have the courage to challenge your convictions.

Identify Barriers to Knowing What You Want

To not know what you want (child model) is easy—if you can be comfortable with the uncertainty. To know what you want (adult model) is not as easy unless you pretend to know, because there are natural and imposed barriers to knowing.

The following are barriers to knowing what you want. Check (✔) the ones that may be your barriers and add others that describe you.

- ❏ I feel paralyzed by the pressure to know what I want
- ❏ I pretend I have a clear goal to "save face"
- ❏ I'm afraid to say "I don't know" when asked "What do you want to do?"
- ❏ I don't have enough experience yet to know for sure
- ❏ I don't have enough facts, and I fear that I cannot get them
- ❏ Predictions about the future keep changing
- ❏ I get conflicting advice from respected advisors
- ❏ What I value is not clear or is conflicting
- ❏ I feel pressure to identify my "destination"
- ❏ Others

_____

_____

_____

These are probably only a few of the barriers to your knowing what you want. Being aware of your personal barriers may help you overcome them. But being flexible—comfortable with the uncertainty of not knowing for sure—can release the pressure to know for sure.

Not knowing what you want is not a serious handicap unless you think it is—in which case you may be so eager to identify what you want that you *pretend* to know, which is a handicap. In setting your goals, positive uncertainty suggests being flexible about your focus. In other words, be focused and flexible about what you want.

Use Goals to Guide You, Not Govern You

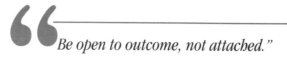

"Be open to outcome, not attached."

—**Angeles Arrien**

One way to find out if what you *think* you want really is what you want is to be uncertain. If you remain unsure of your goals, you will be more likely to reevaluate them frequently and maybe discover new goals. "Try it, you might like it," is what we tell children. You might apply this to yourself and broaden your experiences, expand your interests, and perhaps find new goals.

Have you ever tried something you did not want to do because you had to, and as a result discovered a new joy? If so, describe what happened.

_____

_____

When current events change rapidly, you cannot be sure if where you are going is where you will want to be when you get there. What you want now may not be what you want then.

As George Bernard Shaw pointed out, getting what you want is not always a blessing. Pot-Shots creator Ashleigh Brilliant expresses the feeling that this brings out in a lot of us: "I hope I get what I want before I stop wanting it."

Carly Makes a Surprising Discovery

After graduating from college, Carly decided on a single career goal—to become a chief financial officer. For 12 years she pursued jobs and assignments that would move her closer to her goal. Finally, her efforts paid off and she was promoted to CFO. She was thrilled, but within six months all her joy had disappeared.

Carly dreaded getting up in the morning and was exhausted when she went to bed. She often could not sleep, and she wondered what had gone wrong. She loved the company, the staff, her boss, and the financial rewards of her new job, but she also realized that the job she dreamed of was not what she wanted after all. Carly had let her CFO goal govern her for 12 years. She never questioned whether that goal was still the right one until she achieved it.

Being uncertain of your goals will help you avoid being controlled by them. This strategy allows you to be guided by your goals but not governed by them—open to outcome, but not attached.

Widening Your View of What You Want

Putting blinders on horses' eyes is an example of controlling the focus—making sure that goals govern. Horses' eyes, on the side of their heads, work well for seeing the periphery. Horses are able to see the roses on their journey, so they stop to smell them. But this distracts them from their destination, so blinders are put on to keep them focused. That is what can happen if you are governed by your goals, just like Carly.

In this same way, a zoom lens (being focused) "blinds" your vision of the periphery. And a wide-angle lens (being flexible) allows you to see more than straight ahead. Creative decision-makers, journeying to the future, must be guided by their destinations but capable of being distracted to notice the roses along the side of the road. It means using both the zoom and wide-angle lenses. Being focused and flexible is a *both and more* perspective.

Being goal-guided, not goal-governed, may lead to *serendipity*—a fortunate discovery by accident. Being focused requires you to seek something, and being flexible allows you to be receptive to something else. Maybe it is not just a "happy accident"; maybe the flexibility allowed the discovery. Accidental discoveries cannot happen if you are completely focused on something else.

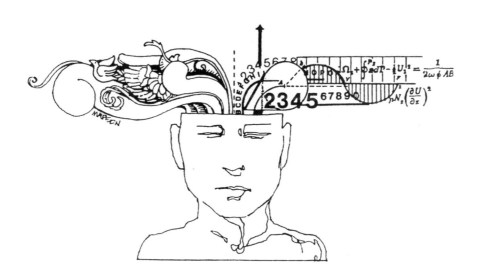

Take Your Eye Off the Target

"
Even in the foreseeable future, there are many things which nobody will have foreseen."

—Ashleigh Brilliant

Keep your eye on the target is conventional wisdom and common sense. But keeping your eye on the target is not wise practice if you are playing tennis—or making decisions. The biggest problem in playing tennis is the normal tendency to look at where you want the ball to go, rather than to keep your eye on the ball. This causes you to miss seeing the ball clearly. Golf presents the same challenge. So does decision making.

Because of the conventional wisdom and the traditional decision strategy about goal setting, the normal tendency of decision-makers, like tennis players and golfers, is to keep their eye on the target, on where they want to go. This causes them to miss seeing the journey clearly. If you keep your eye on the target, you are not likely to discover a new target. You can also be blindsided without your peripheral vision. Practice looking for new goals in every direction.

Keeping your eye always on the target makes you like the horse with blinders. To avoid getting there and finding out that *there* is not where you want to be, take off your blinders and look at the periphery. You might discover another "there" where you would prefer to be. If life is a journey, not a destination, you want to be able to see the journey, to experience all of the territory.

Carly Defines a New Goal

When Carly realized that the target she had worked toward was no longer what she wanted, she took the time to figure out what she did want after all. She identified the work and life interests, values, and skills that were most important to her and analyzed what satisfied and dissatisfied her in her work.

This self-assessment helped Carly rediscover that she liked being a team leader with day-to-day operational responsibilities more than being a financial executive. She disliked the travel and being a key company spokesperson. She also realized that her personal life was different now than when she had first set her goal—now she had a family, a home, and many community interests. She was not the same person she was when she originally defined her goal.

After several months of reflecting on what brought her joy in her work and life, Carly was able to define a new goal—to return to her former role of controller. Rather than leave the company, she decided to propose to her boss, the CEO, that she go back to her old job (a position that was currently open). There was a risk that the CEO would turn down her proposal or lose respect for her, but Carly was willing to take the risk because being unhappy was no longer acceptable.

To her delight, the CEO admired Carly's courage to reconnect with her professional and personal passions, so she agreed to the proposal. The CEO also did not want to lose a valued employee. It turned out to be a win-win for Carly, the company, her family, and her friends. This would not have happened if Carly had not been open to questioning old goals, exploring new ones, and taking the time to figure out what was most important to her.

OPENING YOUR EYES TO OTHER GOALS

Imaginative creativity is helpful for this exercise. Assume you do not have a goal or that there is a very desirable goal out there that you do not see.

Where would you look for this new goal?

_____

_____

What is it that would make a goal very desirable to you?

_____

_____

Are there reasons that you are not able to "see" other desirable goals?

_____

_____

Where are you looking? Are you looking in the wrong places?

_____

_____

Are you unsure what is most desirable to you?

_____

_____

Has someone else already discovered your ideal goal?

_____

_____

Asking yourself these questions, and paying attention to your answers, is part of taking your eye off the target.

Treat Goals as Hypotheses

"Many men go fishing all their lives without knowing it is not the fish they're after."

–Henry David Thoreau

The classical *know what you want* decision dogma prevents us from doubting the one thing about which we probably have the greatest doubts–our goals. Thus, positive uncertainty recommends an experimental approach to goal setting, as suggested by James G. March in "The Technology of Foolishness," in which he says we should treat goals as hypotheses.

A *hypothesis* is something taken to be true for the purpose of investigation. When you decide on a goal, the hypothesis is that you will be pleased when you achieve it. You *believe* the outcome will make you happy. You cannot be certain, of course, until it happens. So you need to investigate.

Imagine the Experiences

Treating goals as hypotheses forces you into futures thinking. Goals and hypotheses are about the future. Treating goals as hypotheses encourages you to use your imagination. You can investigate, in your imagination, if what you think you want really is what you want, before you actually get it. Imagine it happening or not happening, or imagine something else happening. You can even imagine not having a goal and find out how that feels.

In applying positive uncertainty, processing imagination is as important as processing information. The mind does not seem to know the difference between what you experience and what you imagine experiencing. Therefore, if you have a good imagination, you can learn a lot from imagined experiences. You can develop a good imagination by practicing.

Uncover Future Phobia

Future phobia—a fear of exploring the future—is a common barrier to imagining and creating your future. This phobia is characterized by a fear of deciding, of discovering, of being wrong, or of looking stupid. This phobia causes you to avoid creative exploration. It is debilitating because you *let* the future happen rather than trying to make the future happen.

Future phobia causes the decision-maker to dread precisely and dream vaguely, which is a significant barrier to creating the future you want. Your wants are in the future. If you are scared or anxious about the future, then it is difficult to imagine or create a positive future.

To see if you suffer from future phobia, circle the appropriate response to each statement.

I'm anxious that the future won't be what I want it to be so I avoid thinking about it.	Yes	No	Sometimes
I do not have many dreams, goals, or options. My only choice is to keep doing what I'm doing.	Yes	No	Sometimes
The future is not under my control.	Yes	No	Sometimes
People say I am not future-oriented.	Yes	No	Sometimes
I believe the future is random so it doesn't matter what I want.	Yes	No	Sometimes

If you circled *yes* one or more times, you may have a degree of future phobia. This anxiety can prevent you from being creative about what you want, from dreaming impossible dreams, and from discovering new goals.

Developing focus and flexibility and permitting yourself to be comfortable and positive about uncertainty are methods that will help you overcome future phobia.

Your Most Important Life Events

A good memory is important for developing focus about what you want, but it may need creative stimulation. The following is a memory exercise. It is not a test. There are no right or wrong answers. You do not have to share the list; you can change the list; you can list four or seven events rather than five, or whatever number you can quickly jot down. This exercise will help you examine what you want.

List the five most important events in your life. Take no more than two minutes to make your list. Go with what is on the top of your mind.

1. _____

2. _____

3. _____

4. _____

5. _____

Look at your list and determine if it contains recent events or distant events, and events that are positive or negative, career- or family-related, crises or peak experiences, and so on. Your mind remembers selectively, and what it selects to remember is significant. But what it selects to imagine also is significant.

How many of the events on your list are in the future—have not happened yet?

_____

This is not a trick exercise designed to deceive you. Most people do not include important future events on their list. That is one of the insights of this exercise. Isn't it possible that some important event in your life is yet to happen? When we think about our life, we usually think backward.

The Queen in *Alice in Wonderland* said, "It is a poor sort of memory that only works backwards." The dictionary defines memory as the mental faculty of recalling past experiences. And it also defines it as the capacity for storing information. If you could develop a memory that works backward and forward, you would enlarge the size of your memory. You would have more "territory" for collecting information about your wants. You would maximize your capacity to store useful decision-making information.

IMAGINE YOUR FUTURE

To start your memory working forward, list important future events. This list and the past-events list will provide a lot to think about when making decisions.

List the five most important life events in your *future*. Again, take no more than two minutes to make your list. Go with what is on the top of your mind.

1. _____

2. _____

3. _____

4. _____

5. _____

Which is easier for you, remembering the past or imagining the future?

❑ Past   ❑ Future

Why?

_____

_____

Which do you think you know better, your past or future?

❑ Past   ❑ Future

Why?

_____

_____

Think about your answers and why you answered them that way. Most of us have had more practice remembering than imagining. But remembering has as many errors and distortions as imagining. What you "know" about your past may be no more accurate than what you imagine about your future. These two lists, or expanded ones, can be useful in gaining self-understanding and tapping into your creative, futures thinking skills.

Mine Goals from Past and Future Events

> *The pull of the future manifests itself in our lives, our dreams, our hopes, our waves of possible futures."*

—**George Land and Beth Jarman**

The important events of your past and future represent an untapped "goal mine" where you can extract ideas about what is important to you in deciding what you want. You might want to expand both lists to expand your goal mine. What you considered important in your past might help you determine what might be important or unimportant in your future. What you consider important in your future tells you something about possible goals.

Robin Begins to Design Her Life

Robin tried the important life events exercise in a workshop about discovering her work and life passion. In her first list, all the events were in the past. Robin also noticed that the five events were all career focused. This came as a surprise to her. Before then she had not realized that her career had become the defining element of her life.

As she created her important future events list, Robin made a point of thinking about what she wanted for every of aspect of life, not just her career. This exercise helped her take the first step to design, in her words, "my whole life."

Goal mining is a process of looking for goals; it may involve some extra digging and probing. Goals, like gold, are often hidden from view, tucked away in places we seldom look. Sometimes these places are far away, sometimes close at hand. Therefore, we need to search both here (where we are) and there (where we never have been). Goal mining far away and close at hand means using imagination and intuition, using the "pull of the future."

Earlier you were introduced to the three futures—possible, probable, and preferable. This section focuses on the preferable futures—what you prefer to happen. But the "pull of the future" manifests itself in "our waves of possible futures"—what could happen. If you focus too much on the preferable futures, you may miss noticing many of the possible futures. It is in the possible futures where you might extract some preferable futures you did not know about or think about. The goal mining exercise that follows this section will help you broaden your possible images of your preferable futures.

Clarify the Big and Little Things You Want

You can use goal mining to stimulate your creative thinking about what you want for any decision you are making. Start by thinking of the decision as a giant jigsaw puzzle—made up of many pieces, some big and others small. When the pieces are put together, they create a picture; but unlike a jigsaw puzzle, the picture of your decision can change.

For illustration, let's focus on goal mining for your career. To imagine the possible pieces of your career, make two lists—"a little list of big things" and a "big list of little things."

The little list of big things is made up of those parts that take time and effort to achieve, such as promotions, retirement, recognition, financial rewards, and so on. The little list of big things is intended to include a few major factors that are important to you. If you have many, you may need to rank them so you know which are most important or in case they conflict. If you have only a few, make sure you have carefully thought through what is really important to you.

These big things put shape to your career, like the corners or edge pieces of a jigsaw puzzle, but they are not the whole picture. What gives depth and meaning to your career comes from the big list of little things. These are the day-to-day activities that keep you involved, engaged, and motivated. They cover the gamut including what you do in your work, where you do it, whom you work with, how you work, and why. Often the little things are neglected but are as important as the big things in creating satisfaction, happiness, and success in your career.

These little things are important but not "deal breakers." If something is a deal breaker, it belongs on the other list. The absence of a single "little thing" will not spoil your career. But it may be that the absence of many of these little things changes your evaluation of this career. Satisfaction and happiness are made up of both big and little things.

Matt Uncovers a New Goal

Goal mining about big and little things allowed Matt to address his career frustrations. Matt thought he wanted to stop being a sales rep but did not see what other options he had. Matt focused on listing all the little things he wanted in his career and life. This exercise reminded him that what he wanted from his work—meeting with prospective clients and identifying their needs, negotiating and closing deals, selling products he believed in, working with a team he respected—were mostly being satisfied by his current job and company.

As Matt looked at his list again, he saw the one thing that he wanted most was not being satisfied—having flexibility with the hours he worked so he could pick up his daughter from school every day and be involved with her after-school activities. This factor was on Matt's list of little things, but it turned out that it was actually a very big thing.

This goal was so important to Matt that he decided he would take the risk to ask his manager if it was possible to modify his schedule so he could be with his daughter. Matt and his boss negotiated a new work schedule of 6:30 A.M. to 3 P.M., plus Matt agreed to carry his cell phone late in the afternoon in case of an emergency with a prospective client.

Goal mining helped Matt to get more of what he wanted from his whole life, not just his career.

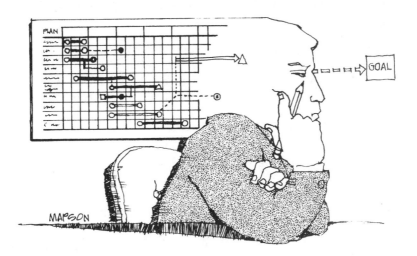

GOAL MINING FOR YOUR CAREER

You can do this exercise on your own or ask others to brainstorm with you. Either way, the objective is to generate many possibilities for your future career. You will have plenty of time later to evaluate the ideas.

1. Imagine it is six months from now. You are feeling satisfied, energized, and motivated by your career. Take your time to picture your career in your mind. You are imagining six months from now as the present. What is happening that is making you happy and satisfied?

   _____

   _____

   _____

   _____

   _____

2. Once you have an image of your future, get more specific by circling those items below that describe what is true for your career six months from now (whether or not it is true today). On the lines that follow, add other items that come to your mind.

Little List of Big Things

➤ I have been promoted.

➤ I have been recognized in my field (or company) for my contributions.

➤ I have reaped financial rewards for my work.

➤ I have returned to school to advance my career.

➤ I have retired to the next phase of my life.

➤ I have stopped working for awhile to pursue other life priorities.

CONTINUED

Add other big things about your career or life that you want to achieve six months from now. If you do not have any, that's fine. At any given time, your career is made up of lots of little things and not that many big things. The key is to know and live what you want.

_____

_____

_____

Big List of Little Things

➤ Most of my day is spent doing work I like to do.

➤ I am using the skills that I most enjoy.

➤ I enjoy the content of my work.

➤ I am learning new skills regularly.

➤ I like what the organization does.

➤ I like the size of the organization.

➤ I work with people I care about and who care about me.

➤ I have a boss who lets me be me.

➤ My work schedule fits well with my personal priorities.

➤ My commute to and from work is manageable.

➤ My work space fits my style.

➤ I am able to satisfy my priorities in both my work and personal life.

➤ The mission of the company fits my interests and values.

➤ I have time and energy to pursue interests outside of work.

Add other little things about what you want to do, where you want to do it, who you want do it with, how you want to do your work, and why you want to work. Be as specific as you can.

_____

_____

_____

Which list was easier to create? Which items are surprising? Why?

_____

_____

Rank both lists; move some from one list to the other; add or subtract some. Perhaps you have been dreaming vaguely. How about dreaming some impossible dreams?

How do you feel about this future career vision?

_____

_____

_____

What new goals have you mined from this future imagining?

_____

_____

_____

_____

This exercise can be modified and expanded to provide other decision-making insights. For example, you might create the two lists for a decision about:

➤ Retirement

➤ A personal relationship

➤ A home purchase

➤ A move to another city

➤ Any decision that is important in your life

When we think of the desired outcomes (our goals), we usually focus on the big things. The big list of little things is an important part of this exercise because little things are often neglected and can be significant to the outcome of a decision.

Postscript

Everyone wants to go to heaven, but no one wants to die."

–James Hillman

You are often told to be careful what you wish for because you might get it. And sometimes the cost of getting the benefits of what you wish for are too high. For example, going to heaven is the goal of many people, but not many are in a hurry to get there or eager to pay the immediate price. Perhaps this should be true of many of our goals in life.

This does not mean you should not have goals or desired destinations. It means to be focused and flexible about them. Know what you want but do not be sure. Realize that the future is unpredictable but persuadable, unknowable but not unthinkable. Where you are going is up to you. Remember, you need to think imaginatively and be creatively persuadable about it.

It is also important to recognize that what you know and believe often determines what you want. At the same time, what you want often influences what knowledge you seek and what you choose to believe.

Talking about what you want separate from talking about what you know and believe is not intended to suggest that they are separate. The complex interconnectedness of these decision factors will be evident throughout this book.

I have learned this at least by my experiments: That if we advance confidently in the direction of our dreams and endeavors to live the life which we have imagined, we will meet with success unexpected in common hours."

–Henry David Thoreau

Paradoxical

Principle #2

This principle will help you both appraise what is known and appreciate the unknown.
What you know may need to become unknown.

30

Be Aware and Wary of What You Know

> *It ain't what you don't know that gets you in trouble; it's what you know for sure that ain't so."*

—Mark Twain

When faced with a decision, the first thing people do is arrange and rearrange what they know. They put their facts in order. If they do not have enough facts, they collect more. Being aware of what you know and knowing more is a good decision-making strategy. But you also need to be wary of what you know, as Mark Twain pointed out. Today's information society produces new knowledge so rapidly that old knowledge becomes obsolete rapidly. This makes it wise to be both aware and wary of what you know.

But being aware and wary of what you do *not* know is also a good decision-making principle—because sometimes what you do not know *does* get you in trouble. The information society has provided more information than ever before. You can know more, but there is also more that you do not know.

With today's pace of discovery and invention of new knowledge, you might agree with Ashleigh Brilliant's observation, "There has been an alarming increase in the number of things I know nothing about." Think of all the new research and inventions that you know nothing about. Being aware and wary makes you a more resourceful decision-maker.

The Tip of the Iceberg

An iceberg might symbolize what you know and do not know. It is well known that about 90% of an iceberg is hidden and that the hidden part is the dangerous part. This represents what you do not know—the part that is often the most consequential. What you know is the iceberg's visible part, and therefore it is the most influential and often deceptive. It can deceive you into thinking you know a lot, yet you may know only 10%.

Applied to decision making, the iceberg metaphor tells us that what we do not know about the possible outcome of any decision (the hidden part) is almost always more than what we do know (the visible part). For example:

> ➤ Before you decide to buy a house, you collect tons of information about the house (roof, plumbing, floors, termites, etc.) but still do not know everything you should. And what you do not know about the neighborhood is even greater.

> ➤ When you decide to start a new job, what you know about the company culture and co-worker personalities is much less than what you do not know and will soon discover.

> ➤ When choosing whom to marry, deciding whether to have children, retiring to a new geographic area, or making any important decision, you should think of the iceberg metaphor and be aware and wary about what you know and do not know.

Facts are part of the picture but they are not the whole scene. Many other factors—including what you want, as discussed in Paradoxical Principle #1—make up the whole picture when making decisions. This part is about facts, information, and what you know. Be aware and wary of your need to know, your need for certainty, and your information anxiety.

Question the Validity of Information You Receive

" *Never ask the barber whether you need a haircut.*"

–Daniel Greenberg

Information is never innocent in the sense of being independent of beliefs, values, or self-interpretation. Information is meaningless (insignificant) until meaning is added by subjective interpretation.

It is easy to see why a barber's advice about a haircut might be biased, but some other subjective interpretations (especially your own) are harder to see. Information you collect is sometimes biased, irrelevant, subjective, incomplete, and maybe even untrue. A lot of this information you did not ask for, did not want, and is not offered in your best interests; and yet it is presented in a psychologically persuasive manner. The world is filled with people who are eager to provide you with information that is in their best interests, not yours.

Kai's Job Interview

Kai was interviewing for a project manager position with an engineering consulting firm. Over the course of a week, Kai interviewed with the president of the firm, three senior engineers, and two vice presidents. Each person was enthusiastic about the company and sold Kai on the job. They all put their best foot forward as they tried to convince Kai to join them and minimized the negative information about the company and the position.

What Kai did not think about is that information involves subjective interpretations and self-interest distortions. Others often distort what they tell you and you often distort what you hear from others. Your mind scans, screens, and selects information. Then you filter and interpret what you allow to get in. While others present information to you in a psychologically persuasive manner, you collect and interpret information in a personally pleasing manner. Leonardo da Vinci said it this way: "All our knowledge has its origin in our perceptions."

Kai's Unfortunate Decision

This is what happened to Kai too. The information he chose to hear during the interviews made him feel optimistic about his career prospects with the company. Kai liked feeling positive so he did not seek out additional information that might change his view. As it turned out, Kai was offered the job and he accepted. Unfortunately, within 90 days of starting, both he and his manager decided they had made the wrong decision. Had Kai sought out more information about management expectations and company culture and been open to collecting negative information, he may well have made a different decision.

You are likely to exaggerate information that supports what you want to know. You may repress or "forget" information that is unfavorable. These deception tricks are crucial to your functioning because to stay sane in the information society, you must scan, filter, and select information constantly coming at you. So you not only get distorted information, you distort it after you get it. Recognize that although knowledge is power, you need to be aware and wary of what you know.

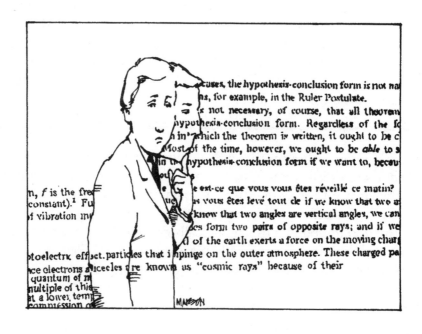

More Information Can Cause More Uncertainty

> **"** *A man with one watch knows what time it is; a man with two watches is never sure."*

—Murphy's Laws

The information collected to reduce uncertainty often increases it. Increasing your knowledge about one possible choice of action may increase the uncertainty about its desirability and also increase the uncertainty of other options.

The reason for the increased uncertainty is that much of the information is contradictory and some of it is no longer true. In today's information society, the half-life of some knowledge is said to be just a few months. As Mark Twain pointed out, what you know that ain't so can get you in trouble when making decisions. Other facts you know can also be confusing, causing uncertainty.

Amy's Search for a Training Program

Amy had been a human resources assistant for a regional bank for three years. She was at a point in her career when she wanted to advance to a management position. To successfully make this move, she needed first to expand her knowledge of the human resources function. Many people advised her to enroll in an HR certificate program.

So Amy began to collect information on HR training programs. She soon found herself in a vicious cycle of collecting information on training programs, feeling confused about what she was learning, and then collecting more information on more alternatives to reduce her uncertainty, which did not happen.

Finally, Amy decided to take a break from the data collection. As she reviewed all the information she had collected, Amy discovered that she was learning about certification programs all over the region. She realized this was not useful information because her criteria were much narrower: a part-time, evening program that was within 30 minutes of her home and work. Once she reminded herself about the most important things she needed to know to make a decision, she was able to narrow the type and amount of information she needed. Then she had a simpler and more doable data collection process, which made it easier to find the training program that met her needs.

Case Study: Coffee Culture

As an example of knowledge's place in decision making, consider what you know about coffee in relation to your decision to drink it. Circle your answers to the following questions:

1. Do you drink coffee?   Yes   No

2. If yes, regular or decaf?   Regular   Decaf

3. How often?   Occasionally Often

4. List the reasons for your answers to the above questions.

_____

_____

_____

5. Is caffeine harmful to one's health?   Yes   No   Maybe

6. Is decaf less harmful?   Yes   No   Maybe

7. Will you drink coffee in the future?   Yes   No   Maybe

Many people make decisions about food consumption from what they know about its effect on health. The reasons for their decisions come from what they read and other sources of information such as advertising or research. Is drinking caffeine harmful to your health? The answer depends on how you make it or take it (not the coffee, the research) and on how much information you have and when you get it. For example, the following is information from caffeine research:

➤ Caffeine may both contribute to heart disease and help alleviate its symptoms.

➤ Caffeine raises, lowers, or does not alter heart rate, metabolic rate, glucose, concentration, and cholesterol levels.

➤ Decaffeinated coffee causes a 7% increase in cholesterol.

➤ Five or more cups of coffee a day, regular or decaf, can cut your risk of colon cancer by 40%.

➤ Drinking coffee does not make people more likely to develop heart disease.

➤ Men who drink decaffeinated coffee, however, show a slightly higher incidence of heart attacks and strokes.

➤ People do die from caffeine overdose.

➤ Caffeine enhances fatty acid metabolism—thus it is used by endurance runners.

➤ Caffeine is widely used in the treatment of headaches.

The research on coffee drinking certainly provides grounds for uncertainty. As you can see, sometimes more information helps to clarify issues, but it also sometimes increases complexity thus increasing uncertainty. And then you ask yourself, "I wonder what I do not know?" or "What do I know that ain't so?"

The problem of deciding about coffee or hundreds of other daily choices is that you often get incomplete, conflicting, irrelevant, or even sometimes incorrect information. And once you have made up your mind, it is hard to change it, even with new information.

Facts about coffee's health benefits and hazards usually do not influence people that much. New evidence about caffeine cannot overcome old knowledge or established beliefs. For some people, cultural indoctrination, personal taste, and acquired habits—rather than information—determine decisions about coffee consumption and many other everyday choices.

Facts are food for thought but they are not the whole meal. Most decisions involve more than research facts. Research itself provides a lot of uncertainty and should be interpreted with caution. For example, recent studies have shown that research causes cancer in mice!

Watch Out for Info-Mania

Info-mania—the idolizing of information—comes from our addiction to the need to know and a feeling of power from knowing. Information anxiety can result from either too much or too little information. *Information Anxiety* author Richard Saul Wurman says, "Information anxiety is produced by the ever-widening gap between what we understand and what we think we should understand. It happens when information doesn't tell us what we want or need to know." And we keep collecting more.

To see if you suffer from info-mania, circle the appropriate response to each statement.

Facts and information make me feel that I have power and control over the future.	Yes	No	Sometimes
Not having lots of information before deciding makes me uncomfortable.	Yes	No	Sometimes
I do not want to look stupid so I collect lots of facts.	Yes	No	Sometimes
People say I am a "just get the facts" type of person.	Yes	No	Sometimes
I believe that the information I need is out there somewhere.	Yes	No	Sometimes

If you circled *yes* one or more times, you may have a degree of info-mania. This anxiety is a leading cause of avoiding uncertainty and inhibiting creativity. The compulsion to know, and the need to disguise not knowing, often hinders learning.

Ignorance may not be bliss, but it is an ideal state from which to learn and get your creative juices flowing. The *both and more* perspective of being aware and wary of what you know not only will make you a more resourceful decision-maker but also may help prevent you from idolizing information—info-mania.

Open Your Mind to New Knowledge

If it can be understood, it is not finished yet."

—Murphy's Laws

We all know that what we know now may not be what we know later. Relevant knowledge lasts for a limited time. Once you think you understand something, you can learn something that changes your mind. What this means is that what you know can change if you are open-minded. If you are closed-minded, old knowledge blocks new knowing.

Open-mindedness may be one of the greatest decision-making skills you can possess. An open mind is receptive. It is a "beginner's mind," a mind that is not full of knowledge, that is continuously learning and changing what it knows. This is empowering because of the tendency for knowledge to keep changing.

The Four Parts of Knowledge

The knowledge you would like to have when making decisions comes in four parts. This is what you would know if you were to make a completely rational decision.

The Four Parts	What You Need to Know
1. Actions	What are the possible actions you could take?
2. Outcomes	What are the possible outcomes of each action?
3. Probability	What is the probability of each possible outcome?
4. Desirability	What is the desirability of each possible outcome?

These four parts are related to the possible, probable, and preferable futures mentioned earlier. Of course because of limited time, limited resources, and limited human rationality, you can never really know all the possible actions, all the possible outcomes, and their probability or desirability when making a decision. And what you do know (or do not know) about each of these parts will change as new events happen, external conditions change, new knowledge is invented, or your personal situation evolves. Thus, you cannot avoid uncertainty about any of these four parts.

But with an open, receptive mind (treating knowledge as changeable), you can be a more resourceful and creative decision-maker by using these four parts as a framework for asking yourself "What else?"

Expand Your Thinking About Other Possibilities

One of the most common pitfalls in good decision making is the failure to consider other possible actions and outcomes. Some reasons for failing to consider possibilities include:

➤ You do not know they exist

➤ You do not want to know they exist

➤ You know the possibilities but "forget"

➤ The possibilities need to be created

Why have you sometimes failed to consider possible actions and outcomes?

_____

_____

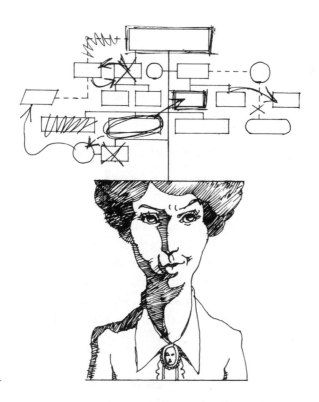

Consider Other Actions and Outcomes

Sometimes not knowing other options or outcomes is okay; sometimes it is disastrous. An open, changeable mind leads to open, suggestible questions about the first two parts of a decision–actions and outcomes. (The other two parts, probability and desirability, are discussed in Paradoxical Principle #4.)

Asking yourself the following questions will help you expand your thinking about possible *actions* you can take:

> ➤ What else could I do?

> ➤ What other possible actions are there?

> ➤ What are the possible alternatives, options, or choices for what I could do?

Asking yourself the following questions will help you expand your thinking about possible *outcomes* that can come from your actions.

> ➤ What else could happen?

> ➤ What other possible outcomes might occur?

> ➤ What are the possible results or consequences of what could happen?

The answers to "what else could I do?" and "what else could happen?" are almost infinite. Sometimes it can be a pitfall to consider too many options or too many outcomes. Then you need to narrow down to make decision making manageable. Still, not knowing about another appropriate career field for you to investigate or another possible positive or negative outcome of your accepting a particular job can be a more serious pitfall.

Sarah's Return to Outside Work

When Sarah's only child began college, Sarah found herself lonely and out of sorts. Her husband was traveling a great deal for work and her son lived 1,000 miles away. She had lots of friends and hobbies but wanted more in her life. She thought that going back to work after 10 years as a stay-at-home mom might be the answer. By asking herself what else she could do besides be a stay-at-home mom, she initially identified three alternatives along with some possible outcomes.

Alternative #1: Return to her former finance career in a full-time capacity. Possible outcomes included:

➤ Upgrading her professional skills

➤ Experiencing career satisfaction again

➤ Not being able to travel with her husband or visit her son whenever she likes

Alternative #2: Work part-time for a small business (which she had done early in her career). Possible outcomes included:

➤ Some flexibility to travel

➤ Time to devote to friends and hobbies

➤ Some structure in her days so she would not feel lonely

Alternative #3: Volunteer part-time for a nonprofit organization (she had always wanted to do this but had never had the time). Possible outcomes included:

➤ Getting to see if she likes working a regular schedule again before committing to a paid job

➤ Developing new friendships

➤ Making a contribution to her community

This exercise got Sarah started in brainstorming her possible futures. It helped her see that she had choices. It also made it easier to describe the possibilities to her friends so they could help her brainstorm more options.

PRACTICE ASKING "WHAT ELSE?"

To help you practice asking yourself what-else questions about actions and outcomes, try this exercise about deciding whether or not to quit your job.

Imagine that you are unhappy with your current job. You need to decide whether to quit or stay—your two decision options.

Assume you are your own decision consultant. Ask yourself the following what-else questions to help you brainstorm other possible actions and outcomes. You are looking for new territory; you want to increase your freedom of choice by seeing other possibilities. There are no right or wrong answers, only possibilities.

What else could I do besides quitting or staying?

List every alternative you can think of (e.g., renegotiate your job, go part-time, etc.). Let yourself be rational, irrational, intuitive, mystical, moral, conservative, risky, practical, foolish, and so on.

_____

_____

_____

_____

Now imagine you have picked the option to quit your job. Answer the following question about possible outcomes of this action.

I've decided to quit my job and be unemployed. What else could happen?

Brainstorm possible positive and negative outcomes that will result from quitting your job and being unemployed (e.g., you'll go on vacation, you'll lose your home, etc.).

_____

_____

_____

_____

=CONTINUED=

Now imagine you have picked the other option to stay in your current job. Answer the following question about possible outcomes for this action.

I've decided to stay in my current job and be unhappy. What else could happen?

Brainstorm possible positive and negative outcomes that will result from your staying in your current job and being unhappy (e.g., you're promoted, you get a new boss, you get sick, etc.).

_____

_____

_____

_____

Having a choice between just two options is not bad if you have narrowed down from many. But to start with two is a deterrent to good decision making. To be wary of what you know means to try to know more. Knowing more possible options and being aware of more possible outcomes is empowering. Learn to ask yourself, "What else?"

ASK "WHAT ELSE?" OF YOUR OWN DECISION

"What else could I do?" (What other actions could I take?) and "What else could happen?" (What other outcomes could result from each action?) are questions that can be applied to every decision.

In this exercise, apply what-else questions to a decision you are currently making or expect to make soon about your career, relationships, education, finances, retirement, and so on. Think of this as personal brainstorming, where you set aside judgment and reality. Forget your previous knowledge, wants, and beliefs–act ignorant.

Describe the decision you need to make:

_____

_____

For this decision, list at least three actions you could consider. Then list three outcomes that might occur for each of the three actions.

What Else Could I Do? **Possible Actions**	**What Else Could Happen?** **Possible Outcomes for Each Action**
1._____ _____ _____	1._____ 2._____ 3._____
2._____ _____ _____	1._____ 2._____ 3._____
3._____ _____ _____	1._____ 2._____ 3._____

CONTINUED

CONTINUED

If you get stuck with this personal brainstorming, do not give up. It is impossible to know everything by yourself. Just as Sarah did, seek out friends, family members, or others who have made a similar decision or are good creative thinkers. Ask them to help you expand what you know. Keep trying to multiply the number of actions and outcomes. See how many more you can identify by continuing to ask the what-else question. The possibilities will increase significantly and so will your creative thinking abilities about what you know.

Postscript

"It is what you learn after you know it all that counts."

—Proverb

What you know is the tip of the iceberg. So what you learn after that is important. What is also important is to acknowledge that what you do not know is the hidden part of the iceberg—the 90% part. It is also important to acknowledge that not knowing—admitting ignorance—can be empowering.

Ignorance is the condition of being uneducated, unaware, or uninformed. To recognize that you are uneducated, unaware, or uninformed is empowering because it can lead to becoming educated, aware, and informed. Philosopher and educator John Dewey explained it another way, "Genuine ignorance is profitable because it leads to humility, curiosity, and open-mindedness." All of these qualities are part of positive uncertainty and lead to learning. Knowing sometimes can be the antithesis of learning.

Remember that what you want and believe partly determines what you know. And what you know partly determines what you want and believe. Knowledge is not wisdom. Be aware and wary of what you know.

"To attain knowledge, add things everyday.
To attain wisdom, remove things everyday."

—Lao tse in the Tao Te Ching

Paradoxical

Principle #3

This principle will help you realize that your beliefs determine both your reality and your behavior.
Believing is seeing is doing.

Be Realistic and Optimistic About What You Believe

> **"** *Everything begins with belief. What we believe is the most powerful option of all."*

—Norman Cousins

What you believe has always been one of the most important factors in what you decide, but it was seldom one of the most important principles of traditional decision strategies. A *belief* is the mental acceptance of and conviction in the truth, actuality, or validity of something. To believe is to have an opinion, to think, to suppose. To believe something is to accept it as real.

Expand the Meaning of Being Realistic

When making up your mind, the typical decision-making battle cry has been, "Be realistic." That is not the wrong battle cry, but it is not the whole battle cry either. Being *realistic* is being aware of things as they really are and having an unbiased awareness—uninfluenced by emotions, feelings, and personal beliefs.

But you really do want emotions, feelings, and personal beliefs to have an influence in your decision making. Positive uncertainty asks you to be realistic in the sense that:

➤ Beliefs are real and they are important

➤ Reality involves more than the outside physical world

➤ Reality is in the mind of the beholder

➤ Reality does not always follow the cause-and-effect rules of empirical science

Add Optimism

Positive uncertainty asks you also to be optimistic. An *optimist* is defined as one who expects a favorable outcome. Why be optimistic? Because:

➤ Optimism is a belief and "everything begins with belief"

➤ Optimists recover faster from illness and injury; perform better at work, in school, and in athletics; and make significantly more money (Martin Seligman, author of *Learned Optimism*)

➤ Optimism and resilience in the face of adversity is the greatest long-term predictor of success for individuals and organizations (Seligman)

➤ An optimistic attitude is the key to persistence and resilience

To be optimistic means that you are influenced by your emotions, feelings, and personal beliefs. To be pessimistic means the same thing. An optimistic or pessimistic belief influences your reality because reality is in the mind of the beholder.

New sciences are telling us that the observer cannot have an unbiased awareness of the reality that is observed. Chaos theory says there is no such thing as objectivity. What is in your mind can become a self-fulfilling prophecy. What you choose to believe is the most powerful option of all.

The decision-making strategies and methods that follow are based on the premise that what you believe determines how you see your reality and that you have a choice about what to believe. To be both realistic and optimistic makes you more than a conventional decision-maker—it makes you a creative decision-maker. It is the *both and more* perspective.

Recognize That Reality Is in the Mind of the Beholder

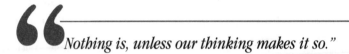

Nothing is, unless our thinking makes it so."

−William Shakespeare

We say beauty is in the eye of the beholder, but we should say that beauty is in the mind of the beholder. What you see as beautiful is not beautiful unless you admire it in your mind. Everyone does not see the same thing as beautiful. This is because believing is seeing. Our beliefs are our spectacles; they show us our reality. Everyone does not see the same reality. The motto of the Scientific School of Police in Paris is: "The eye sees in things what it looks for, and it looks for what is already in the mind."

Psychologist and philosopher William James said, "Our reality is what we attend to... Our beliefs and attention are the same fact." We each choose what to attend to by choosing what to believe.

Beliefs Are the Software of Your Mind's Eye

To use a technology metaphor, your beliefs provide your operating instructions, like the software in the computer. They program what you attend to and therefore what you see. Someone else writes the computer programming; you write the software of your mind by choosing what to believe. Most people make sure their computer software is up-to-date but fail to pay attention to the possible obsolescence of the software that is programming the way they see things.

David Nyberg, author of *The Varnished Truth,* says, "Human self-deception is the most impressive software program ever devised." Actually, this self-selective way of seeing may not be all bad. With so much going on around us, paying attention to everything would be utter chaos. Self-deception (our built-in software) helps us avoid chaos by selecting what to attend to. But it also prevents us from experiencing different ways of seeing. An open mind can expand your experiences and broaden your reality.

Your reality is what *you* believe it to be; it is only *your* reality. The way you see things is not the way everyone sees things. Try the following self-directed interview to learn more about what you believe.

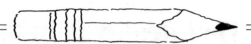

THE SELF-DIRECTED INTERVIEW

An interview is a conversation in which facts and statements are elicited from another. The self-directed interview is a conversation with yourself.

Imagine that you are a talk show host and also the talk show guest. You are interviewing yourself about your beliefs about beliefs. You want to elicit things about yourself that you already know and that you may not yet know. This is part of being reflective and introspective—sometimes called mindfulness.

As a good interviewer, go beyond yes and no or short, uninformative answers. Probe further by asking yourself:

➤ Tell me more

➤ Explain that

➤ Give me an example

Challenge yourself with:

➤ Is that always true?

➤ Would your friends agree?

➤ Is this belief an asset or liability?

➤ Do you want to change that?

➤ Is that your final answer?

Interview yourself using the following questions about your beliefs.

Are you personally responsible for what you believe? If not, who is?

_____

_____

_____

CONTINUED

Are some beliefs better than others?   If so, which ones and why?

_____

_____

_____

What is one of your core beliefs? Where did it come from? Has it ever changed?

_____

_____

_____

Describe a time when one of your beliefs had positive consequences for you and others.

_____

_____

_____

Describe a time when one of your beliefs had negative consequences for you and others.

_____

_____

_____

Bonus question: Do you agree with the following quote by S. I. Hayakawa? Why or why not?

"If you see in any given situation only what everyone else can see, you can be said to be so much a representative of your culture that you are a victim of it."

_____

_____

_____

Be Wary of Your Dogma

"*The surest way to lose the truth is to pretend you already possess it.***"**

—Gordon Allport

Most people hold their truths to be self-evident. This belief can be dangerous because it is a dogmatic belief. Dogmatic believers believe they possess the truth and do not want to lose it by investigating new ideas. "Nothing is more dangerous than an idea when it is the only one you have." (Emile Chartier) If believing is seeing, then the way you see things is the way you see things. Everyone does not see things the same way you do because everyone does not have the same beliefs. Truth is what you can get other people to believe or what other people can get you to believe. In this game of persuasion, *Culture Against Man* author Jules Henry said, "Truth is that which is not legally false."

Replace Dogmatic Believing with Heuristic Believing

Heuristic believing seeks as much to discover, clarify, and understand beliefs as to justify and prove them. Heuristic believers investigate the origin and utility of current beliefs and constantly keep their "software of the mind" up-to-date. Without heuristic believing, the evidence people use to justify their beliefs is often the result of the belief, rather than the cause.

Kevin's Belief About CEOs

Kevin believes that CEOs are autocratic and egotistical. So when he was interviewed by a CEO for a high-level position, Kevin saw the CEO as autocratic and egotistical. If Kevin were the kind who kept checking "the software of his mind's eye," he might have seen that his "believing was seeing" or that he needed more experience with the CEO before making a judgment.

Kevin's belief was his spectacles; he saw what he was looking for. His belief "caused" him to see this CEO in a way that supported his belief. (Of course, it could also be true that this CEO was indeed autocratic and egotistical.)

There is a Zen saying about beliefs and truth: "Believe those who are seeking the truth; doubt those who have found it." To stop seeking the truth makes you closed-minded. Positive uncertainty keeps you open-minded. Be uncertain about your beliefs and be positive about the uncertainty because what you believe in the present was probably established in the past and may need to be revised.

Perceive Perspective Paralysis

Perspective paralysis is the inability to shift your view. People with perspective paralysis are unable to change their perspective. They are stuck in their way of seeing; they have fixed beliefs, hardened attitudes, and concrete convictions. They are dogmatic believers. Perspective paralysis restricts flexibility, adaptability, and, once again, creativity.

To see if you have perspective paralysis, circle the appropriate response to each statement.

I do not believe I have blind spots.	Yes	No	Sometimes
I do not know what my personal beliefs are.	Yes	No	Sometimes
I have deeply held absolute convictions that direct my life.	Yes	No	Sometimes
People say I am closed-minded.	Yes	No	Sometimes
I never think about the consequences of what I believe.	Yes	No	Sometimes

If you have circled *yes* one or more times, you may have a degree of perspective paralysis. Your perspective is your mental map; it comes from your beliefs, attitudes, and convictions. It becomes the way you see the territory.

To be unable to change your mental map of the territory is a disability in a world where the territory is constantly changing. Being a heuristic believer may prevent or cure your paralysis.

Treat Beliefs as Prophecy

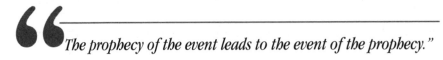

The prophecy of the event leads to the event of the prophecy."

—Paul Watzlawick

The decisions you make today partly determine your future, but they also partly reflect what you believe your future to be. If your future partly reflects what you believe it to be, then what you believe your future to be becomes very important—almost like prophecy. There is probably nothing more powerful, and more empowering, than what you believe about yourself and your future.

When sick people believe they are taking medicine, they often get well, even though what they are taking is only a placebo. The placebo effect arises from the patient's expectations about the treatment rather than from the treatment itself. Beliefs become prophecy.

Positive Illusions and Self-Fulfilling Prophecy

Shelly Taylor's research, which she reported in her book *Positive Illusions,* shows that three adaptive unrealistic beliefs can be positive illusions that create self-fulfilling prophecies. Positive illusions enable people to take action and to manage negative feedback. The three adaptive misconceptions are:

➤ Unrealistic optimism about the future

➤ Exaggerated perceptions of personal control

➤ Unrealistically positive view of self

Rate yourself on the three illusions:

➤ Unrealistic optimism about the future

Low _____High

➤ Exaggerated perceptions of personal control

Low _____High

➤ Unrealistically positive view of self

Low _____High

Your ratings on these illusions will vary according to the decision, the circumstances of the situation, the side of the bed you got up from, and so on. But you may have a certain tendency. A mentally healthy rating is probably not overly high or low.

Taylor's findings contradict many psychologists' and counseling professionals' view that a primary criterion of mental health is an accurate perception of self, of the present reality, and of the probable future. This criterion is clearly changing and raises another paradox: Illusions can be a sign of pathology, or they can make life worth living.

What we now must accept is that denial (refusing to face the facts) and illusions (erroneous beliefs about reality) have their usefulness in coping and may sometimes be the healthiest strategies in certain situations.

Jake's Transition into Public Relations

After a few years of working in marketing communications, Jake became aware that whenever he worked on a public relations project he felt more energized and excited about his work. Plus, he received lots of praise from his boss. So Jake set out exploring what it would take to move into a PR job with his company or another firm.

He learned a lot about the field through online research and informational interviews. Along the way, many people told him that there were few job openings in public relations so it would be like winning the lottery if he found a PR job.

But that information did not stop Jake. A job in public relations was what he wanted and he believed that he could make it happen. He worked hard at developing his skills and making people in the field aware of his goal. After volunteering to do PR for a nonprofit organization for six months, taking evening classes, and networking, he succeeded in finding the job he wanted in another company even though no one believed he could do it—except Jake!

Dream Precisely to Create a Positive Future

Your future reality is partly what you see it to be (the eye of the beholder) and partly what you make it to be (the "I" of the beholder). You can imagine your future by dreaming it and create your future by doing it. Dreaming it is just as important as doing it.

Dreaming vs. Dreading

In Paradoxical Principle #1, dreaming vaguely and dreading precisely were cited in the context of future phobia as barriers to *discovering* what you want. They are also barriers to *getting* what you want.

Dreading precisely gives you clear, detailed negative images of the future. Dreaming precisely gives you clear, detailed positive images of the future. It is very hard to go about creating a positive future if you cannot imagine one. If you improve your dreaming (dream more precisely), you could improve your doing.

Dreaming often gets neglected in decision-making strategies because it is not a rational, left-brain, practical activity. And in school we were not taught dreaming skills and were even told to "stop daydreaming." Yet impossible dreaming, unrealistic optimism, positive illusions, and wishful thinking are all strategies of positive uncertainty because they combine imagery and action, dreaming and doing, the eye of the beholder, and the "I" of the beholder—a *both and more* perspective.

Uncover Your Beliefs Through Metaphor

Metaphors provide a way to uncover your beliefs about how you see things and describe your future from a different perspective. Metaphor is helpful for gaining understanding of something. "It is easier to think about something when thinking about something else than it is to think about a thing when trying to think about it." (Erasmus G. Addlepate)

Beth Looks at Her Life Through Gardening

Beth chose gardening as her personal metaphor for her life. She had a garden in her front yard and backyard. Her front yard was her "public" garden and her backyard was her "private" garden. This made her think about which parts of her life she shared with others and which parts she kept hidden away.

Her front-yard garden was simple and neat—conservative, restrained, not displaying much creativity. But her backyard garden was a hodgepodge of plants that bloomed all year long—an inspired and creative garden.

As Beth thought more carefully about this metaphor, she realized that it was saying that she kept a lot of herself hidden from her friends. In fact, she finally understood what her friends meant when they would say to her, "It seems like you're always holding something back. Let loose! Have fun with life!"

Metaphor Menu

It is helpful if your metaphor is something you are familiar with. Sometimes it helps to pick a metaphor at random or have someone pick one for you. The following menu gives you metaphor ideas that you might apply to your own career, relationships, home, finances, or anything else in your life.

Mountain climbing	Playing the trumpet	*The Wizard of Oz*
Gardening	Software	Computer
Vacation	Dancing	Orchestra
Odyssey	Island	Cabaret
Building a house	Rose	Westward movement
Cooking	Salad	Maze
Tree	Elephant	Bowl of cherries
Golf	"Over the Rainbow"	Game
Passenger bus	Banquet	Stage play
Revolving door	Piece of cake	Journey

Mike Creates a New Metaphor for His Life

After a successful 10-year career with a management consulting firm, things started to go wrong for Mike. He began to feel an exceptional amount of stress and could not sleep or eat.

A friend asked Mike to describe his life in a metaphor. Mike said that it is "a deep hole, with only a tiny light above, and I can't get out even though there's a ladder right next to me." Mike's friend suggested that his metaphor was pretty dark and pessimistic. When he asked Mike if he could change his metaphor, Mike's first reaction was an adamant no!

With coaxing and some help in brainstorming, Mike began to come up with a new metaphor. "My life is like a windy road to the lake and I'm driving on it during a big thunderstorm. I can see blue sky over the ridge and I know that the lake is on the other side—a place that brings me peace and feeds my soul. I want to go there!"

Creating a new metaphor was the first step in Mike's taking back responsibility for his life. It took another year before Mike felt relaxed, focused, and happy again, but he did get there with a new, more optimistic picture of his life.

Explore Your Personal Metaphor

Now is your opportunity to create your own metaphor of the future, or of life if you prefer. Do not worry about being fancy or poetic. If you have never thought of a metaphor for your life, think of this first personal metaphor as a practice.

You can keep changing your metaphor or have different metaphors for different parts of your life or for different times.

Complete this phrase:

My_____ is: _____

         (e.g., job, relationships, life)   (your metaphor)

How is your life like this metaphor?

_____

_____

How is your life *not* like this metaphor?

_____

_____

What does this metaphor say to you about what you want or do not want?

_____

_____

What feelings are associated with your metaphor?

_____

_____

Are you dreading precisely or dreaming precisely in your metaphor?

_____

_____

Do you want to change your metaphor? If yes, what is your new metaphor?

_____

_____

_____

Keep your personal metaphor and work with it, expand it, modify it, change it, or get a new one, as Mike did in the previous example. See if it can give you some insights into your future vision or to help you expand or change your vision.

Use Scenario Rehearsal in Decision Making

A scenario is your vision of an imagined or expected event. Scenario rehearsal is extremely useful in decision making. If you can imagine something happening, you increase your chances of creating it or preventing it.

Using scenario rehearsal also can help you gain insight into your beliefs. Keep asking questions about your visions.

There are three common scenarios you can rehearse for any decision you are trying to make, as follows:

➤ **Best** scenario: the most desirable one you can imagine

➤ **Worst** scenario: the least desirable one you can imagine

➤ **Most likely** scenario: the one you predict will happen

You might wonder, Why describe the worst scenario? Worst-case scenario rehearsal can be useful, although not usually pleasant, because it helps you know if you are dreading more than dreaming, or vice versa. Worst-case scenarios are more likely to be prevented if they are imagined. And not being aware of possible negative outcomes can be hazardous in decision making.

You can change any of your three scenarios with repeated rehearsal. The future does not exist except in your mind. You can become an expert at visualizing any distance with practice exercises about your future beliefs.

Here again is where it might be helpful to have others join in imagining the scenario—best, worst, and most likely. Your family might share their scenarios for next year's vacation. Your friends might share their scenarios for your retirement move to the mountains. Multiple heads are better than one. It helps to have a lot of images about the future. Remember that your decisions about your future partly reflect what you believe it to be.

REHEARSE YOUR OWN SCENARIOS

Describe a decision you need to make:

_____

_____

Now imagine the future *one year from now* in relation to the three scenarios—best, worst, most likely. Describe what each scenario is like, what you are doing, how you are acting and feeling, what you like and do not like, and so on. Describe the scenario in the present tense rather than past tense (e.g., "I *am* doing this" rather than "I *was* doing this.").

1. Describe the *best* scenario: the most desirable one you can imagine.

_____

_____

_____

_____

2. Describe the *worst* scenario: the least desirable one you can imagine.

_____

_____

_____

3. Describe the *most likely* scenario: the one you predict will happen.

_____

_____

_____

_____

CONTINUED

Now examine your three scenarios.

About the **best** scenario:

➤ Was the best scenario easy or difficult to imagine?

❏ Easy   ❏ Difficult

Why?_____

_____

➤ Is it really the best scenario anyone could imagine?

❏ Yes   ❏ No

Why?_____

_____

➤ Is your best scenario overly optimistic or overly pessimistic?

❏ Optimistic ❏ Pessimistic

Explain._____

_____

➤ How did you feel while experiencing the best scenario?

_____

About the **worst** scenario:

➤ Was the worst scenario harder or easier to imagine than the best scenario?

❏ Harder ❏ Easier

Why?_____

_____

➤ Is it really the worst scenario anyone could imagine?

❑ Yes   ❑ No

Why?_____

_____

➤ Is your worst scenario overly optimistic or overly pessimistic?

❑ Optimistic ❑ Pessimistic

Explain._____

_____

➤ How did you feel while experiencing the worst scenario?

_____

About the *most likely* scenario:

➤ Was the most likely scenario easy or difficult to visualize?

❑ Easy ❑ Difficult

Why?_____

_____

➤ What facts did you use to visualize the most likely scenario?

_____

➤ Is your most likely scenario overly optimistic or overly pessimistic?

❑ Optimistic ❑ Pessimistic

Explain._____

_____

➤ How did you feel while experiencing the most likely scenario?

_____

CONTINUED

➤ Was your most likely scenario closest to your best or worst scenario?

❏ Best   ❏ Worst

Why?_____

_____

_____

What does your experience with scenario rehearsal tell you about your beliefs?

_____

_____

_____

This exercise is only one example of using future scenario rehearsal as a decision-making tool. You can imagine scenarios for tomorrow, next week's job interview, next summer's vacation, that important meeting with your staff, winning the lottery, and so on.

Postscript

> ❝*You raise a pup tent from one kind of vision, and a cathedral from another.*❞

—E.B. White

What you believe is such a powerful factor in decision making because what you believe determines your reality and your behavior. Believing is seeing. Edward de Bono, a leading authority on creative thinking, explains, "A belief is an idea, a hypothesis, or a way of looking at the world which forces us to look at the world in a way that supports that belief."

What you believe is, of course, related to what you want and what you know. For example, "One who has a hammer sees the whole world as a nail." (Abraham Maslow)

A person with a hammer wants to see the world as a nail because then he knows what to do. A person who believes her vision of the future is a cathedral will want to know and do things that will help create that cathedral. Creativity involves dreaming and doing and more.

Reality is in the beliefs of the beholder. Optimism is in the beliefs of the beholder. Be realistic and optimistic about what you believe. It is your choice.

> ❝*Reality is what we take to be true. What we take to be true is what we believe. What we believe is based upon our perceptions. What we perceive is what we look for. What we look for depends upon what we think. What we think depends upon what we perceive. What we perceive determines what we believe. What we believe determines what we take to be true. What we take to be true is our reality.*❞

—Gary Zukav, *The Dancing Wu Li Masters*

4

Paradoxical

Principle #4

*This principle will help you use both your head
and your heart in deciding.
What you do to decide is up to you; just do it.*

Be Practical and Magical About What You Do

> "*Rules are for the obedience of fools and the guidance of wise men.*"

–David Oglivy

Paradoxical Principle #4 is about what *you* do to decide what *to* do. It is about the methods, rules, or procedures you use to make decisions.

Many authoritative books and recommended procedures tell you how you should decide. Rules for deciding are found in every bookstore and in many self-development workshops and retreats. People love rules that tell them what to do—and they hate them. It is another paradox. We want to be the captain of our ship, but we also want a pilot's manual.

Being practical and magical is like having a pilot's manual *and* being captain of your ship. The practical, rational procedures for deciding what to do were once conventional wisdom. This is what most people were taught—the pilot's manual. But most people do not practice what is preached—they practice being the captain of their ship.

The Both and More *Perspective*

Positive uncertainty's approach to deciding what to do applies the both and more perspective. It recommends being practical—rational, businesslike, sensible, and reasonable, with down-to-earth thinking. And it recommends being magical—intuitive, mysterious, nonsensical, and playful, with pie-in-the sky thinking. It involves using some rules, breaking some rules, and making up some rules.

To be both practical and magical is to be holistic—whole-brained and whole-hearted. Heart is often defined as the other side of rational, but different from intuitive. It is defined as the source of one's being, emotions, and sensibilities; the repository of one's deepest and sincerest feelings and beliefs; and courage, resolution, and fortitude. The left brain is practical; the right brain is magical. Deciding with the heart is said to be curious, empathic, nonjudgmental, courageous, wise, and compassionate. Thus, the *both and more* perspective calls for using both sides of your brain and all of your heart.

Riley Listens to His Rational and Intuitive Sides

Riley took pride in making rational and logical decisions for all major life choices—buying a car, purchasing a home, relocating to a new state, and accepting job offers—at least until his last job search.

After his company laid off most of the product development department, Riley found himself unemployed for the first time. He felt worried, anxious, and lacking in confidence. He decided he needed to feel more comfortable with uncertainty because of what was happening. Because of the difficult job market, he chose not to spend time gathering and evaluating all the facts about a job offer or to worry about getting the "right" job. Instead, he allowed himself to let his intuition guide him. What he did was play some hunches and go with the flow of the job opportunities that seemed to be available.

After just two interviews, Riley accepted a new position with a small company. He had a feeling this job could evolve into something more, even though he did not have all the analysis to support his hunch.

Riley did not eliminate his rational decision side, but he did not rely on it completely either. This was a big change for Riley. He took a risk and found himself becoming a more versatile decision-maker.

Treat Intuition as Intelligence

 *It is by logic that we prove. It is by intuition that we discover."*

–Henri Poincare

Intelligence is the capacity to acquire and apply knowledge or to use thought and reason. *Intuition* is the ability to know without the use of rational processes, or the knowledge gained from this perceptive insight. Intuition is also called a sense of something not evident, a hunch, an impression, a feeling.

➤ Intelligence is considered left brain—rational

➤ Intuition is considered right brain—nonrational

Intelligence and intuition are beginning to be considered *equally* important mental capacities. Why can't we treat intuition as the "other" intelligence? Why not use the term *intuitive intelligence?*

A Broader View of Intelligence

With his book, *Emotional Intelligence,* Daniel Goleman has done a great deal to broaden our view of intelligence. Think of intuition as right-brain thinking or as part of emotional intelligence. Goleman shows that our conventional view of human intelligence is too narrow, ignoring abilities that matter immensely for what and how we do in life. Emotional intelligence includes:

➤ Self-awareness, self-confidence, and psychological insight

➤ Perspective taking, optimism, and motivation

➤ Ability to accept and initiate change and to handle cognitive anxiety

The intuitive, magical side of decision making is like improvisation. There will be times in your decision making when you will need to improvise—when you have not collected all the facts, when you cannot predict what will happen, and when you do not know for certain what to do. Treating intuition as intelligence will give you permission to improvise.

It should be acknowledged that achieving a both and more wholeness of practical and magical decision making will mean some people will need to build up their respect for and use of logical thinking, the rational intelligence. The reliance on one or the other is not good decision strategy.

Become Aware of Your Decision Strategies

"*Have a place for everything and put the thing someplace else. That's not advice, it is merely custom.***"**

–Mark Twain

Mark Twain makes the point that conventional wisdom and customary practices often are not the same thing. People make rules and then often do not follow them.

Applied to decision making, it can be said that many people claim to use the rational decision method: defining objectives, analyzing alternatives, predicting consequences, and choosing the best alternative (the one with the highest expected value and highest probability and desirability). But they actually use something else. So having a rational decision strategy and using something else is both advice *and* custom.

You, like most people, probably use personal, private decision rules that combine both the rational and intuitive, and more. You, again like most people, probably do not know what your private decision rules are. What you do to make a decision depends on many things, including what you want, know, and believe– positive uncertainty.

Indeed, your decision making should not depend on rigid decision rules. Rules are for guidance, not obedience. You should not become a tool of your rules or a prisoner of your procedures. Every decision is different, so you should become a versatile, creative decision-maker.

Sorting Out Decision-Making Methods

All decision-making procedures, rules, or methods seem to fall into one of the following categories (or a combination). Check (✔) the category or categories that best describe how you make decisions.

❑ *Rational*—"I decide what is best by relating consequences systematically to objectives." ("Ready-aim-fire")

Rational decision making was defined in the first section, which pointed out that humans have limited rationality.

❑ *Intuitive*—"I decide without understanding exactly why." ("Shoot from the hip")

Intuition is not easy to define. The dictionary says it is knowing or sensing without the use of rational processes or a perceptive insight.

❑ *Cultural*—"I decide because that is the way I was taught." ("Standard operating procedures")

Most cultures, societies, or ethnic groups have customs, traditions, or time-honored practices about behavior. These become habits.

❑ *Faith*—"I decide what my religion or spiritual beliefs tell me." ("Do what God, Buddha, or my personal convictions tell me.")

For many people, following their adopted scriptures is their decision rule. Others are defining their own spirituality or their own trusted values and principles for such guidance.

Intuitive, cultural, and faith-based methods are highly idiosyncratic. Until recently, rational rules were the prototype of good decision making. What most people do to decide is private, personal, and unconventional. Private decision rules often escape awareness. These rules start out as guidelines and end up as straitjackets. They often become habits that are too weak to be felt until they are too strong to be broken. Decision-makers can help themselves by checking their unnoticed decision habits, by becoming aware of their private decision rules.

Julie Chooses a College

An example of an idiosyncratic decision strategy is the way Julie chose her college. Her guidance counselor advised her to research colleges by their reputation, majors she was interested in, cost, and the like—all rational factors for choosing a college.

When Julie found herself deciding between two colleges, the decision came down to four factors:

➤ Distance from home

➤ Quality of the school

➤ Proximity to skiing

➤ Beauty of the campus

Julie did a pros and cons list for each school and assessed what would likely be satisfying and dissatisfying about each choice. When it finally came to making her decision, she went with her intuition. When she compared the beautiful color brochure of one college to the black-and-white brochure of the other, she knew the college photographed in color was the right place for her. Her mother thought her decision making was flawed (but then, her mother wanted her to go to school close to home). In the end, though, Julie was happy with her choice and comfortable with how she made it.

Paradoxical Principle #4 does not intend to prescribe a better rule for deciding what to do. It encourages decision-makers to develop a repertoire of decision strategies—like playing golf. A golfer has a bag of clubs and selects a different club for different shots, depending on many factors. A decision-maker has a repertoire of decision strategies and selects a different strategy for different decisions depending on different factors. Positive uncertainty encourages decision-makers to develop a "big bag" of different decision strategies. Then you can choose from your bag of decision strategies the one that is appropriate for where you are on the "course" and that fits the way you intend to "play this hole."

GO HABIT HUNTING

A habit is a recurrent, often unconscious pattern of behavior. Because we do not see these habits, it might be wise to hunt for them. Habit hunting is the process of looking for your unconscious patterns of decision-making.

The following habit-hunting exercise will point out your decision methods that may have become unnoticed habits. This is often difficult to do because sometimes we really do not know how we decide and because the way we think we should decide and the way we do decide are often different.

Describe one decision you have made recently.

_____

Check (✔) the decision methods you recall using to help you make the decision:

❑ Play it safe: I chose the alternative with the least risk

❑ Go for it: I chose what could lead to the best outcome, regardless of the risk

❑ Escape catastrophe: I chose what was most likely to avoid the worst possible outcome

❑ Impulsive: "Ready-Fire-Aim"

❑ Procrastinate: "Ready-Aim-Aim-Aim..."

❑ Do different: I chose the path less chosen

❑ Fatalistic: I left it up to fate to decide—"It is in the cards"

❑ Compliant: I let someone else decide—"Whatever you say"

❑ I chose by the seat of my pants, top of my head, shot from my hip

❑ I did what the Bible or other Scripture said to do

❑ I did what God, Buddha, or other spiritual leader would do

❑ I chose what my inner voice told me, what felt right

❑ I did what my parent, boss, or other authority figure told me to do

❑ I followed my culture's custom—my standard operating procedures

❑ I let my values guide me

❑ I added up the pros and cons to decide

=CONTINUED=

List other decision methods that you used to make your decision.

_____

_____

Why did you decide that way?

_____

_____

Describe the way others might have decided.

_____

_____

What do you believe is the correct way to decide? Or what is the best way?

_____

_____

What is your most common way to decide?

_____

_____

What have you learned about your decision habits?

_____

_____

Go habit hunting regularly to be aware of, understand, and expand your decision rules. Augment your habit hunting by sharing your answers with others that know you well. Ask them for feedback on how they see you making decisions. This can be an enlightening experience.

Recognize Reverse Paranoia

Paranoia is the belief that someone is following you and out to get you. Reverse paranoia is the belief that you are following someone who is out to lead you. Reverse paranoiacs are looking for that visionary leader. Reverse paranoiacs not only want the "white knight" to lead them to the Promised Land; they want him to visualize it for them. Reverse paranoia is a disability because it stifles self-reliance.

To see if you suffer from reverse paranoia, circle the appropriate response to each statement.

I'm scared that I will make the wrong decision.	Yes	No	Sometimes
People say I do not usually decide for myself. I expect others to do the deciding for me.	Yes	No	Sometimes
Self-reliance is not one of my strengths.	Yes	No	Sometimes
I like having precise, authoritative rules for deciding.	Yes	No	Sometimes
I do not like being "captain of my ship."	Yes	No	Sometimes

If you circled *yes* one or more times you may suffer from a degree of reverse paranoia. This disability leads to reactive behavior rather than proactive behavior. Reverse paranoiacs do not believe they are responsible for creating their own future.

Self-reliance is one of the key skills in the future workplace and in all areas of life. Taking charge of your own decision rules helps prevent or overcome this paranoia. What you decide is up to you. Just do it.

Learn to Plan and Plan to Learn

"The best-laid plans of mice and men are usually about equal."

–Murphy's Laws

Common wisdom says that before you do anything you first should have a plan. But it may be that the planning process is more important than the plan itself. You probably have heard the popular saying, "Life is what happens to you while you're making other plans." Murphy's Law above reflects the typical value of most of our best-laid plans. Life is what happens to us—so let's learn from it. Learning from experience is powerful; the only thing more powerful is not learning from experience.

The Paradox of Designing and Discovering

Learn to plan and plan to learn is another paradox.

> ➤ To plan is to design—that is, to design a course of action

> ➤ To learn is to discover—that is, to discover new knowledge or new experiences

If you focus only on the design, you may fail to discover. Thus, be focused *and* flexible.

A plan is a scheme or method designed in the present but intended to culminate in the future. When you make a plan you assume the present conditions will remain the same. And you also assume the plan's purpose will remain the same. But things change. And your plan may need to change. So let what happens to you be a lesson to you.

Learn to plan is wise advice. It involves setting goals, designing strategies, and projecting probable outcomes. Much has been written about the value of learning how to plan. This is not obsolete, but it is insufficient. Learning how to plan is only a beginning.

Plan to learn also is wise advice. It involves discovering new goals, revising former strategies, and visualizing other possible outcomes. Today, current conditions do not stay the same very long. Using both sides of planning will make decision making a process of both designing and discovering.

Dan's Transition into New Work

Dan had been supervising a curriculum design project in the school district for three years and really enjoyed what he was doing. He had worked long and hard to get to this point of his career and felt that he had finally "arrived."

Then unexpectedly the school district found itself operating in the red and needed to cut the budget. Dan was one of the first to be laid off. He was stunned. Everything he had planned for was now over, or so he thought.

After a month or so of reeling from the shock, Dan began talking with friends about what other job possibilities he might look into. As he began to learn what other people were doing and about available job opportunities, he discovered a new direction—instructional design for a corporate training department.

After looking into this path more carefully, Dan found that this could be a good, new career direction for him. He launched a full-scale job search and after several months found a new job with a new future. Dan learned that planning is good but he also learned to expect to change his plans—something he had not thought about before.

Visualize Outcomes with Decision Trees

The decision tree is a graphic representation of the four parts of a decision, which were covered in Paradoxical Principle #2. As a reminder, the four parts are:

The Four Parts	What You Need to Know
1. Actions	What are the possible actions you could take?
2. Outcomes	What are the possible outcomes of each action?
3. Probability	What is the probability of each possible outcome?
4. Desirability	What is the desirability of each possible outcome?

One decision tree represents one possible action. The trunk of the tree is the action and the branches are the outcomes. Every decision has several possible actions, thus several decision trees. The following is an example of the four parts of a decision illustrated in a decision tree with two options–two decision trees.

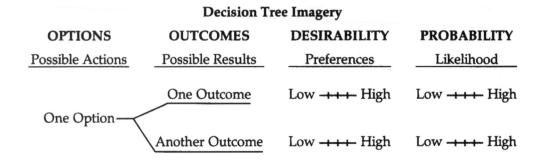

Decision Tree Imagery

If you can plant such decision tree imagery in your mind's eye (so that it is always there), it can be useful in developing your repertoire of decision strategies for big or small decisions. This decision tree imagery gives you a visual starting point. Using this visual model, you can bounce between the rational and intuitive methods and decide what to do when you feel ready or when you must.

You can, of course, draw the picture each time you face a decision and fill in the blanks for that particular decision, using many decision trees and branches for all the options and outcomes.

See the Bigger Picture in Outcomes Windows

Paradoxical Principle #2 focused on asking what-else questions to brainstorm actions and outcomes. The *outcomes window,* as illustrated in the exercise that follows, helps you ask what-else questions about the *desirability* and *probability* of possible actions and outcomes. But the outcomes window model does not stop there. It asks you to identify positives and negatives for you *and for others* who may be affected by the option.

Claire Considers a New Career Opportunity

Claire was director of quality assurance for a major computer software company. A career opportunity that she dreamed of was about to come true, but it required relocation to a different part of the country. Claire felt pretty certain that she would accept the job but she wanted to be sure before saying yes to her boss.

First, she analyzed the pluses and minuses of the work. Then she took the time to fill in the outcomes window, a decision-making technique she had learned in a workshop. Claire listed the positive outcomes as career success and financial security (she would get a significant raise and bonus). When she listed the negative outcomes, she realized they were all personal—missing her family and friends, leaving the town she grew up in and loved, and having a hard time meeting new friends because she felt shy. This exercise reminded Claire of one of her most important values—having close personal relationships.

As Claire reflected on the possible outcomes for others, she thought of her husband, Harry. On the positive side, he would be closer to his best friend and he loved new adventures, which this move certainly would be. On the negative side, he might not find a new job.

The outcomes window exercise helped Claire to see that this decision involved more than career advancement. She intuitively knew this, but writing down all the possible outcomes for herself and her husband brought her decision making more into focus.

You can enhance the value of the outcomes window by getting others' opinions of what you put in, what you left out, and so on. Even ask others to fill in the outcomes window about the option from their perspective and then compare your results.

Claire Makes Her Decision

At the end of the day, Claire took home the results of the outcomes window exercise to show her husband. He was very happy to see that she was taking the time to analyze the decision and suggested that he complete the exercise from his perspective.

Harry agreed with most of Claire's outcomes but added a few more. He did not imagine the negative outcome of his not finding a new job. In fact, his company had an office in a town nearby so he might even be able to get a transfer. About the negatives, he saw many more. Harry was an only child and his parents lived nearby. He was very close to them, as was Claire. His dad had recently been diagnosed with Alzheimer's disease. If Harry and Claire moved away, Harry felt that his mom would be overburdened with the caretaking responsibility and would risk getting sick herself. Harry also imagined that he and Claire would not be able to buy a home like the one they currently had and loved.

When they compared their results, they realized that the job was a fabulous opportunity but there was more to their life than work. They decided that the time was not right to move to another part of the country. As a result, Claire turned down the transfer this time, but kept her eyes open for a new opportunity closer to home. She and her husband felt good about their joint decision making.

As you have seen for Claire, using the outcomes window when making significant life decisions helps you develop a larger picture of the probability and desirability of possible options and outcomes.

OUTLINE YOUR DECISION IN THE OUTCOMES WINDOW

Describe a decision you need to make:

_____

_____

In the windows below, list all the possible positive and negative outcomes for you and others who will be affected by this decision.

	Positive Outcomes	**Negative Outcomes**
Self		
Others		

Are some segments of the outcomes window less full than others? If so, why? They could all be full if you worked on it more.

_____

_____

Was it easier to think of positive or negative outcomes? Why?

_____

_____

Whom did you consider as "others"? Did you overlook some?

_____

_____

═CONTINUED═

Which is more important: outcomes to you or to others?

_____

_____

Rank the positive and negative outcomes by importance.

_____

_____

Now think about the probability (likelihood) of these outcomes.

What is the likelihood that each of your high-priority positive or negative outcomes would occur? (Indicate high, low, medium, or 75%, 50%, 25%, etc.)

_____

What evidence did you use for these estimates?

_____

_____

How does the probability affect your decision making?

_____

_____

Are you a risk taker? A risk avoider? Risk taking often depends on the degree of desirability of outcome.

_____

Probability estimates come from information and from your subjective interpretation. A completely rational process would ask you to multiply probability times desirability to get a quantitative criterion. Because such a criterion is so complex and unreliable, you might use what-else questions, decision tree, or outcomes window methods to come to a practical and magical decision.

INTERNAL DEBATE: LOGICAL OR INTUITIVE?

Sometimes you may want to be very logical when deciding what to do. Other times you may want to use a more intuitive approach to deciding. Many times it will be a combination, your combination. A way to find the right combination of logical and intuitive is with the internal debate exercise. Have a dialogue with yourself about the different sides of each option—the logical, rational side and the intuitive, magical side.

Describe a decision you have already made or will make soon:

_____

_____

On the lines below, list everything you can think of in support of the option, using each side of your brain. Then list the people who would support each side.

Rational and Practical Reasons That Support This Decision	**Intuitive and Magical Reasons That Support This Decision**
_____	_____
_____	_____
_____	_____
People Who Would Support the Rational Side	**People Who Would Support the Intuitive Side**
_____	_____
_____	_____
_____	_____

CONTINUED

How do you feel about each argument?

_____

_____

_____

_____

Also notice who is on each side. What kind of people are they? Does their opinion matter? Would you like to be more like them? What does their position tell you?

_____

_____

_____

_____

Decisions are not made by information or analytical models, but by people. More information and more analysis is not always the answer. Sometimes you have to make a choice somewhere between rational and intuitive. Make it with positive uncertainty.

Postscript

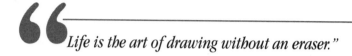

"Life is the art of drawing without an eraser."

–John W. Gardner

Nowadays it is not said very often that life is a science. Now living as art is a common metaphor. We see book titles such as *The Art of Problem Solving, The Art of Making a Living, Composing a Life, The Art of Happiness,* and *Leadership Is an Art.* Art brings out images of creativity, virtuosity, dexterity, skill, cunning, sensitivity, and imagination. Drawing without an eraser brings out images of making lots of mistakes.

Creative decision making with positive uncertainty is the art, not the science, of making decisions. It involves creativity, virtuosity, dexterity, skill, cunning, sensitivity, and imagination. And it involves making a lot of mistakes. It says to let life be a lesson to you. Or as someone explained it, "Life is like playing a violin solo in public and learning the instrument as you go along."

The point in decision making is that you always have to make choices without knowing what the results will be. That is, you must learn as you go along. As one of Murphy's Laws points out, "In any given circumstance, the proper course of action is always determined by subsequent events."

Positive uncertainty's decision-making advice has been to act like a child, use metaphor as method, try not to know a lot, use your genuine ignorance, keep changing your mind, take some risks, embrace uncertainty, accept paradox. In other words, make mistakes and learn.

Conventional wisdom says, " It is better to have tried and failed than never to have tried at all." Positive uncertainty says, "It is better to have tried and failed than never to have failed at all."

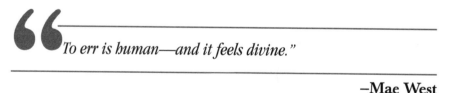

"To err is human—and it feels divine."

–Mae West

S U M M A R Y

Actions for Practice

Actions for practice summarize the key concepts of positive uncertainty and provide you with a checklist of actions you can take to develop your skill at creative decision making. Keep this summary handy and refer to it whenever you need to make a significant career or life decision.

1. Embrace the four paradoxical principles.

Positive uncertainty is a decision-making philosophy. It recommends that you acknowledge and be positive about uncertainty. The four paradoxical principles provide opportunity for creativity and proactive behavior.

✔ Be focused and flexible about what you want.

✔ Be aware and wary about what you know.

✔ Be realistic and optimistic about what you believe.

✔ Be practical and magical about what you do.

2. Shift from *either/or* to *both and more.*

The *both and more* position is another paradox and provides a holistic perspective to decision making. For example, it says to be both a thinker and a feeler at the same time. To be both seems contradictory yet might be more than being either/or.

✔ Use your whole brain; be both rational and intuitive.

✔ Use all your senses, your head, your heart, your gut, the seat of your pants, and so on.

✔ Develop a memory that works in both directions—remember the past and imagine the future.

✔ Make sure your idea is not the only one you have. Multiple options are empowering.

3. Be aware of the software of your mind's eye.

The way you see things is the way you *choose* to see things. You are the developer of the software of your mind's eye. Believing is seeing. It is up to you.

✔ Learn to dream positively and precisely.

✔ Employ metaphor, creativity, and scenario rehearsal as decision-making tools.

✔ Have the courage to challenge your convictions.

✔ Watch for personal warning signs of the four new neuroses: future phobia, info-mania, perspective paralysis, and reverse paranoia.

4. Become a futurist.

All decisions are about the future. Your decisions partly determine your future and partly reflect what you believe your future to be. Think creatively about the three kinds of futures:

✔ The *possible* futures: This is what you think could happen.
Become a "possibilist," imagine as many possible futures as you can.

✔ The *probable* futures: This is what you expect will happen.
Remember that what you expect is influenced by what you want, believe, and do not know.

✔ The *preferable* futures: This is what you want to happen.
Treat your preferable futures as hypotheses—let goals guide you, not govern you.

Think of the future as unpredictable but persuadable. Focusing too much on the probable and preferable futures may cause you to miss some possible futures—where the creative opportunities reside.

The Perennial Decision-Making Question

Here is a make-believe decision-making question-and-answer interview. This could represent the ultimate decision-making question and the ultimate decision-making answer.

The question comes from Alice when she meets the Cheshire Cat at a fork in the road in the classic book, *Alice in Wonderland:*

"Which way should I go from here?"

The answer comes from Jon Kabat-Zinn in the title of one of his best-selling books:

"Wherever you go, there you are."

Whenever you face an important decision and wonder, "Which way should I go from here?" remember to tell yourself, "Wherever I go, there I am."

Positive Uncertainty Exercises

What follows are the positive uncertainty exercises that can be used again and again as you make significant decisions. Think of these as resources for future applications. The following exercises are included:

Paradoxical Principle #1: Be Focused and Flexible About What You Want

➤ Goal Mining Exercise

Paradoxical Principle #2: Be Aware and Wary of What You Know

➤ Ask "What Else?" Questions

Paradoxical Principle #3: Be Realistic and Optimistic About What You Believe

➤ Explore Your Personal Metaphor

➤ Scenario Rehearsal Exercise

Paradoxical Principle #4: Be Practical and Magical About What You Do

➤ Outline Your Decision in the Outcomes Window

➤ Internal Debate: Logical or Intuitive?

GOAL MINING EXERCISE

Goal mining is a process of looking for goals; it may involve some extra digging and probing. You can use goal mining for any decision you are making to stimulate your creative thinking about what you want.

Define the decision: _____

_____

Now define the outcome you want. This is your goal, your preferable future, your most desirable image or vision, your best scenario. Take the time to picture your future in your mind. Imagine it has happened.

Describe your preferred outcome:_____

_____

_____

_____

In the boxes below, create two lists. Write in the present tense (e.g., "I am..." or "I like...") rather than past tense (e.g., "I was..." or "I did...").

1. A little list of big things (important, high-value events or feelings) that describe what is true now that your vision is reality

2. A big list of little things (important day-to-day activities) that describe what you are doing, how you are feeling, and so on

Little List of Big Things	**Big List of Little Things**
_____	_____
_____	_____
_____	_____
_____	_____
_____	_____
_____	_____
_____	_____

═CONTINUED═

Which list was easier to create? Which items are surprising? Why?

_____

_____

Rank both lists; move some items from one list to the other; add or subtract some. Perhaps you have been dreaming vaguely. How about dreaming some impossible dreams?

Now, how do you feel about this vision now that you are there?

_____

_____

What, if any, new goals have you mined from this future imagining?

_____

_____

_____

_____

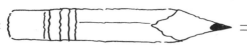

ASK "WHAT ELSE?" QUESTIONS

The purpose of this exercise is to help you avoid the common pitfall of failing to consider possible actions and outcomes. You probably cannot think of them all, but to think only of a few limits your decision-making capability.

Apply what-else questions to a decision you are making or expect to make soon. Think of this exercise as personal brainstorming, where you set aside judgment and reality. Forget your previous knowledge, wants, and beliefs—act ignorant.

Describe the decision you need to make:

_____

_____

For this decision, list a *minimum* of three actions you could consider. Then list a *minimum* of three outcomes that might occur for each of the three actions. Ask others to help you think creatively. Of course, there are many more than three actions and three outcomes. The more you can think of, the more possibilities you have.

What Else Could I Do? **Possible Actions**	**What Else Could Happen?** **Possible Outcomes for Each Action**
1._____	1._____
_____	2._____
_____	3._____
2._____	1._____
_____	2._____
_____	3._____
3._____	1._____
_____	2._____
_____	3._____

EXPLORE YOUR PERSONAL METAPHOR

Metaphors provide a way to describe your future from a different perspective and uncover your beliefs about how you see things.

Complete this phrase (using your job, life, future, family, or anything familiar):

My_____is _____

(e.g., life)   (your metaphor, e.g. a three-ring circus)

How is your life like this metaphor?

_____

_____

How is your life *not* like this metaphor?

_____

_____

What does this metaphor say to you about what you want or do not want?

_____

_____

What feelings are associated with your metaphor?

_____

_____

Are you dreading precisely or dreaming precisely in your metaphor?

_____

_____

Do you want to change your metaphor? If yes, what is your new metaphor?

_____

_____

_____

SCENARIO REHEARSAL EXERCISE

A scenario is your vision of an imagined or expected event. You can rehearse the following three common scenarios for any decision you are trying to make:

1. **Best** scenario: the most desirable one you can imagine

2. **Worst** scenario: the least desirable one you can imagine

3. **Most likely** scenario: the one you predict will happen

Scenario rehearsal is extremely useful in decision making. If you can imagine something happening, you increase your chances of creating it or preventing it.

Describe a decision you need to make:

_____

_____

Now, imagine the future *one year from now* in relation to the three scenarios—best, worst, most likely. Describe what each scenario is like, what you are doing, how you are acting and feeling, what you like and do not like, and so on. Describe the scenario in the present tense rather than past tense (e.g., "I *am* doing this" rather than "I *was* doing this").

Describe the *best* scenario: the most desirable one you can imagine

_____

_____

_____

_____

Describe the *worst* scenario: the least desirable one you can imagine

_____

_____

_____

_____

═CONTINUED═

Describe the *most likely* scenario: the one you predict will happen

_____

_____

_____

_____

You might wonder, Why describe the worst scenario? Worst-case scenario rehearsal can be useful, although not usually pleasant, because it helps you know if you are dreading more than dreaming, or vice versa. Worst-case scenarios are more likely to be prevented if they are imagined.

Now examine your three scenarios.

About the ***best*** scenario:

➤ Was the *best* scenario easy or difficult to imagine?

❑ Easy   ❑ Difficult

Why?_____

_____

➤ Is it really the best scenario anyone could imagine?

❑ Yes   ❑ No

Why?_____

_____

➤ Is your best scenario overly optimistic or overly pessimistic?

❑ Optimistic ❑ Pessimistic

Explain._____

_____

➤ How did you feel while experiencing the best scenario?

_____

CONTINUED

About the *worst* scenario:

➤ Was the worst scenario harder or easier to imagine than the best scenario?

❑ Harder ❑ Easier

Why?_____

_____

➤ Is it really the worst scenario anyone could imagine?

❑ Yes   ❑ No

Why?_____

_____

➤ Is your worst scenario overly optimistic or overly pessimistic?

❑ Optimistic ❑ Pessimistic

Explain._____

_____

➤ How did you feel while experiencing the worst scenario?

_____

About the *most likely* scenario:

➤ Was the most likely scenario easy or difficult to visualize?

❑ Easy ❑ Difficult

Why?_____

_____

➤ What facts did you use to visualize the most likely scenario?

_____

106

➤ Is your most likely scenario overly optimistic or overly pessimistic?

❑ Optimistic   ❑ Pessimistic

Explain._____

_____

➤ How did you feel while experiencing the most likely scenario?

_____

➤ Was your most likely scenario closest to your best or worst scenario?

❑ Best   ❑ Worst

Why?_____

_____

_____

What does your experience with scenario rehearsal tell you about your beliefs?

_____

_____

_____

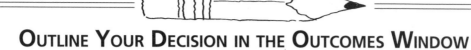

OUTLINE YOUR DECISION IN THE OUTCOMES WINDOW

The outcomes window helps you ask what-else questions related to the desirability of the possible outcomes. But the exercise does not stop there. It asks you to identify positives and negatives for both you *and others* who may be affected by the option.

Describe the decision you need to make:

_____

In the windows below, list all the possible positive and negative outcomes for you and others who will be affected by this decision.

	Positive Outcomes	**Negative Outcomes**
Self		
Others		

Review your completed outcomes window. Remember, you are looking for insight.

Are some quarters of the outcomes window less full than others? If so, why? They could all be full if you worked on it more.

_____

_____

Was it easier to think of positive or negative outcomes? Why?

_____

_____

=CONTINUED=

Whom did you consider as "others?" Did you overlook some? Did you ask for their input?

_____

_____

Which is more important, outcomes to you or to others?

_____

_____

Rank the positives and negatives by importance.

_____

_____

Now think about the probability (likelihood) of these outcomes.

What is the likelihood that each of your high-priority positive or negative outcomes will occur? (Indicate high, low, medium, or 75%, 50%, 25%, etc.)

_____

What evidence did you use for these estimates?

_____

_____

How does the probability affect your decision making?

_____

_____

Are you a risk taker? A risk avoider? Risk taking often depends on the degree of desirability of outcome.

_____

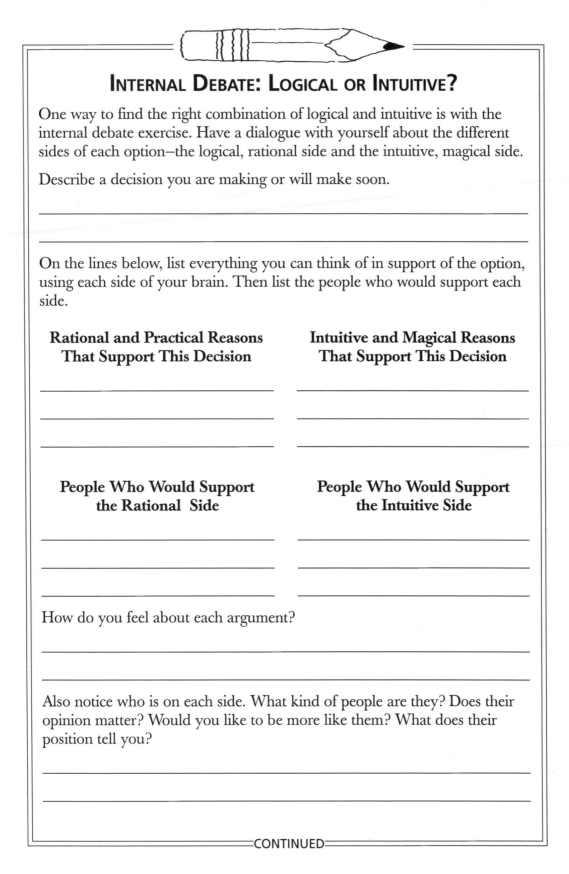

INTERNAL DEBATE: LOGICAL OR INTUITIVE?

One way to find the right combination of logical and intuitive is with the internal debate exercise. Have a dialogue with yourself about the different sides of each option—the logical, rational side and the intuitive, magical side.

Describe a decision you are making or will make soon.

_____

_____

On the lines below, list everything you can think of in support of the option, using each side of your brain. Then list the people who would support each side.

Rational and Practical Reasons That Support This Decision	**Intuitive and Magical Reasons That Support This Decision**
_____	_____
_____	_____
_____	_____

People Who Would Support the Rational Side	**People Who Would Support the Intuitive Side**
_____	_____
_____	_____
_____	_____

How do you feel about each argument?

_____

_____

Also notice who is on each side. What kind of people are they? Does their opinion matter? Would you like to be more like them? What does their position tell you?

_____

_____

Recommended Reading

Csikszentmihalyi, Mihaly. *Finding Flow*. NY: Basic Books, 1997.

Feldman, Daniel. *Critical Thinking*. Menlo Park, CA: Crisp Publications, 2002.

Goleman, Daniel. *Emotional Intelligence*. NY: Bantam Books, 1995.

Harman, Willis. *Global Mind Change, Revised Edition*. San Francisco: Berrett-Koehler, 1998.

Kindler, Herb. *Clear and Creative Thinking*. Menlo Park, CA: Crisp Publications, 2002.

Kindler, Herb. *Risk Taking, Revised Edition*. Menlo Park, CA: Crisp Publications, 1999.

Seligman, Martin. *Learned Optimism*. NY: Alfred Knopf, 1991.

Taylor, Shelley. *Positive Illusions*. NY: Basic Books, 1989.

Zukav, Gary. *The Seat of the Soul*. NY: Simon & Schuster, 1989.

Selected Articles by H.B. Gelatt

Collard, Betsy and Gelatt, H.B. "Beyond Life Quality: The Integration of Work and Life." In *New Directions In Career Planning And The Workplace,* 2000. Second Edition, Edited by Jean M. Kummerow. Davies-Black Publishing, 2000. Reframes the work-life balance crisis.

Gelatt, H.B. "Future Sense: Creating the Future" in *THE FUTURIST,* Journal of the World Future Society. Sept.-Oct. 1993. (www.wfs.org) Defines the four neuroses that inhibit creativity: Future Phobia, Info-Mania, Mind's Eye Myopia, and Reverse Paranoia.

Gelatt, H.B. "Positive Uncertainty: A New Decision-Making Framework for Counseling" in *Journal of Counseling Psychology,* Vol. 36, No. 2, 252-256, 1989. (www.apa.org) Describes the changes from a rational framework to a *both and more* decision-making model.

Now Available From

THOMSON
™
COURSE TECHNOLOGY

Books•Videos•CD-ROMs•Computer-Based Training Products

If you enjoyed this book, we have great news for you. There are over 200 books available in the *Crisp Fifty-Minute™ Series*. For more information contact

Course Technology
25 Thomson Place
Boston, MA 02210
1-800-442-7477
www.courseilt.com

Subject Areas Include:

Management
Human Resources
Communication Skills
Personal Development
Marketing/Sales
Organizational Development
Customer Service/Quality
Computer Skills
Small Business and Entrepreneurship
Adult Literacy and Learning
Life Planning and Retirement